Dancers

OF THE BALLET

BIOGRAPHIES

by MARGARET F. ATKINSON

and MAY HILLMAN

DANCERS
OF *THE* *BALLET*

NEW YORK: *Alfred A. Knopf*

The authors and publisher wish to give credit as follows for the photographs used to illustrate this book:

Gordon Anthony, London: *Elaine Fifield* [bottom of page 53]
Studio Armand, Havana: *Alicia Alonso* [page 9]
Ballet Theatre: *Hugh Laing* [page 89]; *Nora Kaye* [page 81]
Baron: *Yvette Chauviré* [bottom of page 25]; *Marjorie Tallchief* and *George Skibine* [page 153]
Leslie Caron: *Leslie Caron* [top of page 21]
Larry Colwell: *Ruthanna Boris* [page 17]
Constantine: *Alexandra Danilova* [page 37]; *Mary Ellen Moylan* and *Oleg Tupine* [page 117]; *Mia Slavenska* [page 145]
Denis de Marney: *Elaine Fifield* [top of page 53]
André Eglevsky: *André Eglevsky* [page 49]
Samuel Goldwyn Productions, Inc.: *Renée Jeanmaire* & *Roland Petit* [p. 79]
Harcourt, Paris: *Leslie Caron* [bottom of page 21]
George Karger, Pix, Inc.: *John Kriza* [page 85]
Serge Lido, Paris: *Jean Babilée* [page 13]; *Leon Danielian* [page 33]; *Colette Marchand* [page 107]
Lipnitzki, Paris: *Serge Lifar* and *Yvette Chauviré* [page 103]
Studio Liseg, Paris: *Anton Dolin* [page 43]; *Rosella Hightower* [page 75]
Metro-Goldwyn-Mayer Studios: *Moira Shearer* [page 137]
Walter E. Owen and New York City Ballet: *Diana Adams* [pages 2 and 5]; *Janet Reed* [page 129]
Walter E. Owen: *Yvonne Chouteau* [page 29]; *Tanaquil LeClercq* [page 93]; *Maria Tallchief* and *Francisco Moncion* [page 149]; *Maria Tallchief* [page 151]
Carl Perutz-Magnum Photos, New York: *Robert Helpmann* and *Margot Fonteyn* [page 71]
Carl Perutz-Magnum Photos, Paris: *Roland Petit* [page 125]
Rothschild Photo by Maxine Reams, Los Angeles: *Les Sylphides* Ballet Russe de Monte Carlo [title page]
Richard Sasso: *Jocelyn Vollmar* [page 165]
Seeberger, Paris: *Yvette Chauviré* [top of page 25]
Maurice Seymour: *Alexandra Danilova* [jacket]; *André Eglevsky* [page 51]; *Margot Fonteyn* [page 57]; *Frederic Franklin* [page 63]; *Beryl Grey* [page 67]; *Alicia Markova* [pages 109, 111]; *Nina Novak* and *Leon Danielian* [page 121]; *Tatiana Riabouchinska* and *David Lichine* [page 97]; *Yvette Chauviré* and *Oleg Tupine* [page 161]; *Igor Youskevitch* [page 167]; *Tatiana Riabouchinska* and *Adolph Bolm* [from the collection of *Dance News*] [page 133]; Nina Novak and Leon Danielian [back of jacket]
Twentieth Century-Fox Films: *Tamara Toumanova* [page 157]
Alfredo Valente: *George Skibine* and *Alicia Markova* [page 141]
Wide World Photos: *George Zoritch* and *Denise Bourgeois* [page 171]

THIS IS A BORZOI BOOK, PUBLISHED BY ALFRED A. KNOPF, INC.

This title was originally catalogued by the Library of Congress as follows:

927.933 Atkinson, Margaret Fleming. Dancers of the ballet; bibliographies of Margaret F. Atkinson and May Hillman (pseud.)

1. Dancers. I. Hipshman, May B., joint author.

L.C. Catalog Card Number: 53-7624   ISBN: 0-394-91066-4 (Lib. ed.)

AUTHORS' NOTE

Among ballet-goers, each of whom has his own favorite dancers, personal preferences are a matter of heated debate. No two ballet fans anywhere would agree on a list of the world's greatest dancers, nor does this book attempt arbitrarily to establish such a list. Because of limited space, many fine dancers of international repute have regretfully been omitted, and the book has been confined to a cross section of the leading ballerinas and *premier danseurs* of the United States, England, and France. In most cases, these are the stars whom the average American is likely to see—on tour, in the movies, or on television. All of these dancers have an important place in the vital art that is ballet today.

ACKNOWLEDGMENTS

To the many dancers, both in the United States and in Europe, who patiently answered questions and generously lent irreplaceable photographs, the authors owe their deepest gratitude.

We are especially indebted to the following people for their invaluable assistance in gathering material and interviewing dancers: John Hobart in Paris, Isabel Rae and Veronica Johns in New York, and Betty A. Ferrell in Los Angeles; and we are grateful to Martha McGahan and Ralph Gleason for their editorial assistance.

We wish also to thank the directors, managers, and press departments of Ballet Russe de Monte Carlo, Ballet Theatre, New York City Ballet, L'Opéra Paris, Sadler's Wells Ballet, Sadler's Wells Theatre Ballet, Metro-Goldwyn-Mayer Studios, Samuel Goldwyn Studios, Twentieth Century-Fox Films Corporation and United Artists Corporation for their co-operation in furnishing material and photographs, and in some cases arranging interviews.

Our appreciation to the ballet authorities: Mme Irène Lidova in Paris, Arnold Haskell in London, and Anatole Chujoy in New York, for their help and counsel.

Grateful acknowledgment is made to John Masefield, Poet Laureate of England, and to William Chappell for permission to reprint excerpts from their writings.

Acknowledgment is also made to the numerous photographers whose photographs are herein reproduced; especially to Serge Lido in Paris, Baron in London, Maurice Seymour in Chicago, and Walter E. Owen in New York.

THE MAKING OF

a Ballet Star

Almost every little girl, after seeing her first ballet, dreams of herself as the ballerina—that fairy-like creature who shimmers in the spotlight's fire. And almost every mother, watching her little daughter make up her first steps to the radio, is carried away with rosy visions of her child as the great star of tomorrow. So strong is the lure of ballet that thousands of little girls all over the world start to ballet school each year—and from these thousands perhaps fifty will emerge as tomorrow's ballerinas, and one may rise above all the others as a star of the first magnitude, to take her place among ballet's immortals: Pavlova, Karsavina, Taglioni.

What makes a ballerina? Is she born with her dazzling talents? And how has she developed them? Where did she begin?

She begins as a small girl—usually between eight and ten *—to take her first ballet lesson. She starts out with one lesson a week, and at the end of two years will probably have progressed to a daily lesson. She will continue to take a lesson every day for the rest of her dancing life, even after she is a star. By the time she is sixteen or seventeen, she is ready to begin her career as a professional.

What has our dancer learned during these long years of preparation? Primarily, she has acquired a thorough training in ballet technique—the control of the muscles of her body, enabling her to perform all the difficult, traditional ballet positions and movements. If she is fortunate, she has studied with a really great teacher, formerly a great dancer, who has passed on to her the rich traditions of ballet, and has guided her in a study of the arts to which ballet is closely allied: music, literature, and painting. Above all, she has learned that mere mastery of technique is not enough—that the ability to do an *entrechat-six* or thirty-two *fouettés* does not make her a fine dancer, any more than brilliant five-finger exercises make a concert pianist.

Thus equipped, our young dancer is ready to look for a job. She finds a place in the *corps de ballet* of a well-established company, and is now officially a ballet dancer—but far from a ballerina. She will appear only as one of the group of dancers who form a sort of chorus in ballet. Though she herself has little chance to shine, she can study at close range the soloists and ballerinas whose roles she hopes some day to dance.

She goes through periods of deep discouragement, when she feels sure she will be in the *corps de ballet* for the rest of her life. Then, unexpectedly, she is told to understudy a solo role! Sometimes luck gives her a hand: the regular soloist falls ill, or leaves the company, and our dancer goes on in her place. It is a beginning, but her one solo does not make her a soloist. Only after she has

---

* Ballet authorities agree that eight to ten is the ideal age for little girls to start ballet training. Earlier than that can cause actual physical harm to young muscles and bones, and after twelve the young body is no longer flexible enough.

danced many solo roles of increasing importance and variety will she have earned the title of soloist.

As a soloist, our dancer begins to get her first notice from the critics. The company's ballet master, who has been watching her carefully, and considers her a dancer of promise, eventually lets her understudy a ballerina role. Or perhaps the choreographer, working on a new ballet, decides to try her out in a small leading part.

That glorious night when she appears on stage in her first ballerina role seems to our blissful dancer the reward for all her years of hard work and dreams. But that performance, so earth-shaking to her, may pass quite unnoticed by the critics. She is not yet, by any means, a ballerina. A dancer seldom leaps to fame in a single performance, or even in a single season. If she has proven adequate in her first ballerina role, she is given another, and then another. Only after she has danced leading roles regularly for several seasons does she reach the goal on which her eyes have been set over the long years. She is a ballerina.

There are, of course, rare cases in which a dancer wins fame overnight. Perhaps once in a decade a new ballet is an instant sensation from the moment the curtain rises at the *première*, and the leading dancer, who has had the luck to dance a role that especially shows off her individual talents, is swept to immediate fame along with the ballet. Such instantaneous acclaim was won, for example, by Nora Kaye in *Pillar of Fire*, and by Leslie Caron in *La Rencontre*.

There are even rarer cases in which a dancer is endowed with such extraordinary talents that she seems destined for greatness from the time she first begins her training. The career of such a dancer follows no pattern, for fame unerringly singles her out wherever she may be. She is the great dancer. She is the one who moves her audience to tears, to wild applause, to adoration. There are but a few of her caliber in the whole world during any century. Today, critics agree on only a handful of such dancers: Alexandra Danilova, Alicia Markova, Yvette Chauviré, Margot Fonteyn, and Maria Tallchief.*

The *premier danseur*, partner of the ballerina, holds a position of importance equal to hers. This handsome gentleman, elegant in tights and tunic, may appear to the average ballet-goer to have little to do but lift the ballerina around, and stand back in admiring attitudes. But there is far more to his role than meets the untrained eye.

To be a fine partner is an art that takes years to develop. It is not just a matter of being strong, or masculine, or possessing a perfect technique. The art of partnering is the art of showing off the ballerina to the audience in such a way that she appears perfection itself. The *premier danseur* uses his strength to lift her as though she were a feather; his masculinity to emphasize her delicate airiness; his technique to make hers the more dazzling. The ballerina owes much of her success to his skillful, deferential handling of her.

---

* Galina Ulanova, Russia's outstanding ballerina since 1938, is often included in this group of the world's "greats." The brilliance of her dancing, which had been only a rumor in the Western world, was well established when she was allowed to dance in Florence in 1950, and when press representatives were permitted to visit Moscow's famous Bolshoi Theatre for the first time in 1953.

The great *premier danseur* frequently shows himself a more spectacular dancer than his partner when his turn comes to dance alone. In a *pas de deux* or a *variation,* he performs feats of agility—mighty leaps, brilliant *entrechats,* incredible *pirouettes*—that win him his just share of the applause. The famous demi-character roles, in which he can display his acting ability as well as his technique, give the male dancer his best opportunity to shine on his own. Ballet repertoires abound in such roles: the Miller in *The Three-Cornered Hat,* the Peruvian in *Gaité Parisienne,* the Polovtsian Chief in *Prince Igor,* the sailors in *Fancy Free*—all are tremendous display pieces for the male virtuoso.

The training of a *premier danseur* is as complete and arduous as that of the ballerina, and follows much the same pattern. He may not begin so young as she, but he goes through the same basic training in the background of ballet and in the traditional techniques, with one exception—he will probably not dance on *pointes.* This delicate, airy technique is generally used only by female dancers, with a few notable exceptions, such as Anton Dolin's hair-raising solo on *pointes* in *The Fair at Sorochinsk.*

Ordinarily, his training and advancement go more speedily than a ballerina's. It is not unusual for a male dancer to be accepted as a member of a company's *corps de ballet* after only two or three years of training, and after that he may make startlingly rapid progress to top rank. Today there is a crying need for virile young men in the ballet companies of the world, and for that reason almost any boy with an athletic background and a reasonably attractive face and physique can achieve success as a dancer within a relatively short time.

But to achieve true greatness as a *premier danseur* requires not only exceptional talents, but long years of experience and maturity. Among contemporary dancers, too many of whom are more concerned with showing off their own prowess than with showing off their partner, the really outstanding classical *premier danseurs* can be counted on the fingers of one hand: Anton Dolin, André Eglevsky, Robert Helpmann, Michael Somes, and Igor Youskevitch. These men, all at the peak of their artistic maturity, are the brilliant exponents of a rapidly disappearing art—the art of partnering.

THE MAKING OF

a Ballet

A ballet, in which the ballerina and her partner play the stellar roles, is much more than just dancing. It is the combination of four arts: dancing, music, drama, and painting—the work of many individuals, most of whom the audience never sees. The music to which the dancers move, the theme of the ballet, the sets and costumes, are just as much a part of the finished production as is the dancing itself. The perfect fusing of all these ingredients, adding up to a single over-all effect, is ballet.

Blending these arts into an harmonious whole is the work of the choreographer. He is, first of all, the composer of the dancers' movements—creating the series of steps and patterns which will form his ballet. To add to the complexity of his art, the choreographer must see that the movement and music seem made for each other, and that the sets and costumes, while heightening the effectiveness of the ballet, do not detract from the dancers themselves.

The really great choreographer is a rare being, for he must be an artist of the front rank. In addition to being a thoroughly trained dancer, he needs wide knowledge of music, literature, and painting. He must possess a fertile imagination, an original mind, and a deep understanding of human nature.

In international ballet today, the greatest name is unquestionably that of Leonide Massine, dancer and choreographer *extraordinaire*. Ever since 1914, when he did his first choreography for the Diaghilev Ballets Russes, he has dominated the ballet scene in Europe and America. He is recognized as a choreographer of dynamic originality, an actor-dancer without peer, and a teacher and ballet master who has molded many of today's finest dancers.

Among his many contributions to choreographic art, Massine's greatest is the Symphonic Ballet. His *Les Présages*, to Tschaikovsky's Fifth Symphony; *Choreartium*, to Brahms's Fourth Symphony; and *Seventh Symphony* to Beethoven were the first brilliant examples of what is today accepted as a separate ballet form.

Massine has greatly extended the range of ballet, introducing subjects that are today in common use: folk-dancing and national music, great paintings, historical events, and modern life. He also enriched ballet with a variety of extraordinarily detailed character roles. The Peruvian in his *Gaité Parisienne*, the Miller in *The Three-Cornered Hat*, the Hussar in *Le Beau Danube* are warmly developed, three-dimensional characters, the like of which ballet had never known before.

Massine, whose brilliance as a dancer and inventive genius as a choreographer have illumined the ballet scene for the past forty years, still remains a giant in contemporary ballet.

In American ballet, which is enjoying a golden era, the leading figure today is George Balanchine, artistic director and choreographer-in-chief of the New York City Ballet. Under his strong direction that company, in existence only since 1948, has already become the largest and most vigorous company in the United States.

George Balanchine, a Russian-born dancer and musician, joined the Diaghilev Ballets Russes in 1924, at the age of twenty, and it was in that company that his genius as a choreographer was first evidenced. From the time he came to the United States in 1934, he has been vastly influential in shaping the whole course of American ballet.

Together with Lincoln Kirstein, he was co-founder of The School of American Ballet, the American Ballet Company, Ballet Caravan, Ballet Society, and the New York City Ballet. Each of these organizations was a logical outgrowth of its predecessor, and each more firmly established the individual character of ballet in America. For all of these companies, Balanchine has done prolific and inspired choreography, marked by two distinguishing characteristics: his neo-classicism, typical of which are his *Orpheus, Firebird,* and lovely *Sylvia pas de deux,* and his development of ballets of almost pure abstract dance pattern (as in his *Concerto Barocco, Ballet Imperial,* and *Capriccio Brillant).* He has also greatly enriched the symphonic ballet, especially with his *Theme and Variations* to Tschaikovsky, *Symphonie Concertante* to Mozart, *Palais de Cristal* (now called *Symphony in C)* to Bizet.

Balanchine is also largely responsible for the introduction of ballet into musical comedy and light opera. His choreography for *On Your Toes, I Married an Angel, Babes in Arms,* and *Louisiana Purchase* started a trend which today has reached such proportions that a musical comedy without a ballet scarcely seems complete. His dances in *Rosalinda, The Merry Widow, Song of Norway,* and *The Chocolate Soldier* did much the same for light opera.

Balanchine's greatness as a choreographer is so interrelated with his greatness as a director, organizer, and teacher that it is impossible to separate them. George Balanchine and American ballet are virtually synonymous.

Antony Tudor, English-born dancer and choreographer, has also played an important role in the development of ballet in America. He made his American debut with Ballet Theatre in 1939, and with his first psychological ballet, *Pillar of Fire,* in 1942 was instantly established as a choreographer of great stature. *Pillar of Fire* remains one of the most remarkable ballets in the whole American repertoire, and in it Tudor's genius for drama and character development were brilliantly evidenced. His ballets—among them *Jardin aux Lilas, Dim Lustre, Undertow,* and *Romeo and Juliet*—have given individual dancers more opportunity to display their own depth of interpretation and feeling for drama than has the work of any other choreographer. The dancer-actor, epitomized by Nora Kaye and Hugh Laing, came into his own in the ballets of Antony Tudor. Since he has been in the States, he has worked with several companies, and continues to enrich American ballet with his perceptive and warm understanding of human nature in such of his outstanding recent ballets as *Lady of the Camellias* and *La Gloire.*

Jerome Robbins's name is known to every American theater-goer for the remarkably spirited ballets he has created both for the ballet stage and for Broadway musicals. The first sensational success of this native New Yorker was the ballet *Fancy Free,* which he did for Ballet Theatre in 1944. It was expanded the same year into a highly successful musical, *On the Town,* and later remade into a movie of the same name. Robbins's reputation as a choreographer was heightened with his later work for Ballet Theatre: *Facsimile* and *Interplay.* He is producing some of the New York City Ballet's most original ballets: *The Pied Piper, Age of Anxiety,* and *The Cage*—called his most powerful and mature work to date. His success has been just as outstanding in the field of musical comedy. His warmly humorous ballets for *High Button Shoes; Look, Ma, I'm Dancing!; Call Me Madam;* and *The King and I* have established Robbins as one of Broadway's top choreographers.

Agnes de Mille, another noted name among American choreographers, has won substantial acclaim for her ballets of the native American scene. Her *Rodeo,* produced by Ballet Russe de Monte Carlo in 1942, introduced the Western cowboy to the ballet stage, and was such an instant hit that Miss de Mille shortly afterwards did the tremendously successful choreography for *Oklahoma!* In that musical, her ballet *Laurie Makes Up Her Mind* was the first in musical comedy history to form a part of the actual plot, instead of being an unrelated interlude. New York-born Agnes de Mille, niece of Cecil B. de Mille, did her first choreography in Europe. Since 1940 she has been guest choreographer for Ballet Theatre, and her distinguished ballets include *Black Ritual, Tally-Ho, Fall River Legend,* and *The Harvest According.* The witty sophistication of her choreography has enlivened many of the biggest musicals since *Oklahoma!*: *One Touch of Venus, Carousel, Bloomer Girl, Brigadoon,* and *Allegro.*

There are many other important American choreographers, whose ballets are seen from coast to coast: Lew and Willam Christensen, founders, directors, and choreographers of the San Francisco Ballet since 1937; William Dollar, John Taras, and Todd Bolender, who form what might be called the Balanchine school of choreography; Ruth Page, whose *Frankie and Johnny* is particularly memorable; Michael Kidd, noted chiefly for his *On Stage!* and choreography for the musical *Finian's Rainbow;* Eugene Loring, whose *Billy the Kid* is a standard favorite with Ballet Theatre; Ruthanna Boris, currently producing for the New York City Ballet. These American choreographers, utilizing to the fullest the technical brilliance and showmanship of American dancers, are creating many of the most provocative and soundly original ballets to be seen anywhere in the world.

Ballet in England today is dominated by the tiny, dynamic figure of Dame Ninette de Valois, co-founder and director of Sadler's Wells Ballet, Sadler's Wells Theatre Ballet, and the associated Sadler's Wells Ballet School. Through her devoted work in both companies and the school, she has developed a truly national ballet in England. Her influence as a teacher, director, and choreographer is profound.

Miss de Valois was already a dancer of note when she opened her own small ballet school in 1926, to train English dancers. She was active at the same time as both dancer and choreographer in the struggling young Camargo Society and Ballet Rambert. In 1931, she opened a second school at the Sadler's Wells Theatre, from which eventually grew the two companies that now form the backbone of English ballet, ranking among the world's finest. Miss de Valois, who has a genius for discovering and developing young talent, has produced at least one dancer of international stature—Margot Fonteyn. All of England's top ballerinas—Beryl Grey, Moira Shearer, Elaine Fifield among them—have been trained in her school and graduated into the Sadler's Wells Ballet or Theatre Ballet.

One of England's first choreographers, and one of the few major women choreographers in ballet's history, Miss de Valois has created a score of distinguished ballets, including *Job, The Rake's Progress, Promenade, Orpheus and Eurydice,* and *The Prospect Before Us.* So high is the esteem in which she is held by her countrymen that she was decorated by the late King George for her outstanding contributions to English ballet.

Frederick Ashton, currently chief choreographer of Sadler's Wells Ballet, has produced a large number of works noted for their elegance, theatrical effectiveness, and originality. He has created more than fifteen ballets especially for the company's leading ballerina, Margot Fonteyn, which give her talents far wider expression than does the work of any other choreographer. Among his most outstanding ballets (many of which were seen in the United States during the company's three tours from 1949 to 1954) are: *Lilac Garden, Les Patineurs, Les Rendezvous, Façade, Dante Sonata,* and *Symphonic Variations.* Among the ballets he has done for other companies are: *Devil's Holiday* for Ballet Russe de Monte Carlo, *Illuminations* and *Picnic at Tintagel* for the New York City Ballet.

In France, where ballet today is enjoying a real renaissance, the two foremost choreographers are Serge Lifar, director of the Paris Opéra, and Roland Petit, now directing his company Les Ballets de Paris. Both men are also dancers of extraordinary talents, and for that reason their stories appear in the main part of this book, along with other dancers' biographies.

We have seen that there is far more to ballet than meets the eye. There is the lengthy, demanding training of the dancer, the long-established traditions and techniques that govern ballet, and the work of the unseen artists—chief among them the choreographer.

There is one final and essential ingredient of any ballet performance—the audience, each member of which plays a dual role, for he is both spectator and critic. The more he knows about ballet—what the dancer is trying to do, what the choreographer is seeking to express, what part the other artists have played—the more he will get out of the performance in appreciation and enjoyment. And the more he knows, the better the performance the dancers will give, for they can be completely inspired only by an enlightened audience who will be satisfied with nothing less than the dancers' best.

Learning to be a well-informed ballet-goer is a rewarding hobby, for to the balletomane the whole enchanting and beautiful world of ballet lies open each time the curtain rises on a new performance.

Contents

THE MAKING OF A BALLET STAR   vii

THE MAKING OF A BALLET   ix

Diana Adams   3

Alicia Alonso   7

Jean Babilée   12

Ruthanna Boris   16

Leslie Caron   19

Yvette Chauviré   23

Yvonne Chouteau   28

Leon Danielian   31

Alexandra Danilova   35

Anton Dolin   42

André Eglevsky   48

Elaine Fifield   52

Margot Fonteyn   55

Frederic Franklin   61

Beryl Grey   65

Robert Helpmann   69

Rosella Hightower   74

Renée Jeanmaire   77

Nora Kaye   80

John Kriza   84

Hugh Laing   88

Tanaquil LeClercq   92

David Lichine   96

Serge Lifar   101

Colette Marchand   105

Alicia Markova   108

Mary Ellen Moylan   115

Nina Novak   119

Roland Petit   123

Janet Reed   127

Tatiana Riabouchinska   131

Moira Shearer   135

George Skibine   140

Mia Slavenska   144

Maria Tallchief   147

Marjorie Tallchief   152

Tamara Toumanova   155

Oleg Tupine   159

Jocelyn Vollmar   163

Igor Youskevitch   166

George Zoritch   170

SOME BALLET TERMS AND WHAT
    THEY MEAN   173

INDEX   follows page 174

Dancers

OF THE BALLET

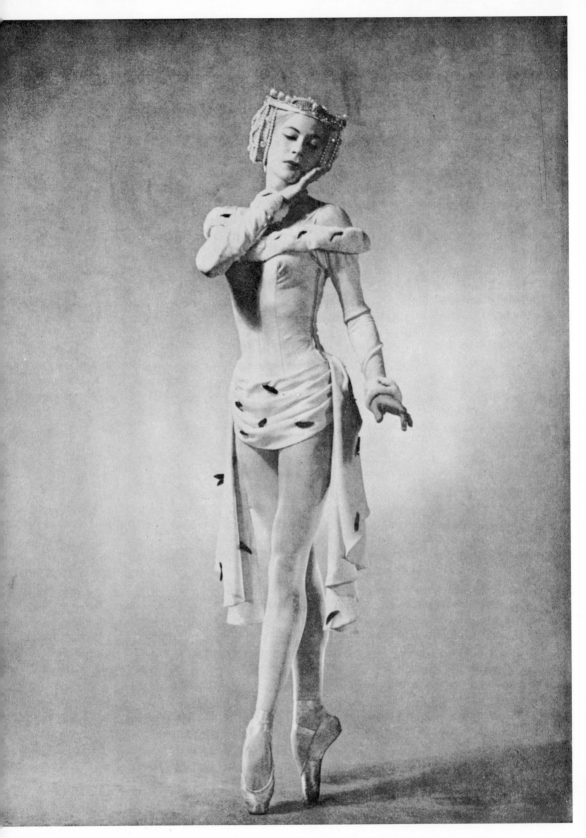

DIANA ADAMS as Iseult in *Picnic at Tintagel*

Diana Adams

To watch a ballerina dance is to be caught up in a moonlit world of magic and enchantment. This fragile and ethereal being, whirling in such airy grace, looks as though she must sleep on a cloud and live solely on rose petals and champagne. But the days when the great ballerinas drifted in an aura of glamour, surrounded by admirers offering diamonds and chateaux, are gone forever.

Today's ballerinas lead workaday lives like the rest of us. They are people with a job, unusually attractive people working at unusually demanding jobs, which take up all their time. Although their financial rewards are small, their rewards as artists are so keenly satisfying that not one of them would willingly exchange her life for any other.

What is a ballerina's life really like? This question is often asked of Diana Adams, tall, curly-haired ballerina with the New York City Ballet. She answers it readily in her charming voice with its trace of soft, Southern accent. She's up every morning at eight-thirty in the midtown New York apartment where she and her husband, *premier danseur* Hugh Laing, live. She fixes orange juice and coffee, does the dishes, walks the dog. Then she and Hugh catch a bus to the Metropolitan Opera House for the ballet lesson that is part of every dancer's daily routine. At noon they have a quick counter-lunch at the drug store, then go to City Center for rehearsal with the New York City Ballet, which may last from two to four hours, depending on the schedule. She does the marketing, has a short rest if there is time, then a light snack, and is back at the theater by six-thirty. She warms up at the practice *barre*, does her elaborate make-up, gets into costume, and is ready for the performance at eight-thirty. Afterwards, except on the rare occasions when there is a party for the cast, she and Hugh go straight home, tired and hungry, but still keyed up by the night's performance. Gradually, as they fix and eat their late dinner, the one big meal of the day, they begin to relax, and by midnight are ready for bed.

When they do manage a day to themselves, they sometimes spend it at the beach, but more often they loaf about the apartment. Hugh putters with his furniture-making, Diana with her sewing and short story writing.

This is the pattern of Diana Adams's life for most of the year, but occasionally it is broken by tours of the United States and Europe. Once she had a glorious vacation with her husband in Barbados, the beautiful West Indies island where he was born. But most of the time she lives in a fixed round of class, rehearsal, and performance which is typical of the lives of dancers.

This routine is automatic for Diana, who has been a professional dancer since she was sixteen. She was born in Staunton, Virginia—a Southern background that may account for her air of almost old-fashioned sweetness. Her father was an English teacher, and her stepmother, Mrs. Emily Hadley Adams (a former ballet dancer), had a ballet school of her own. It was inevitable that little Diana should start to study ballet when she was old enough. At seven, in Memphis, Tennessee, she started lessons with Mrs. Adams willingly enough, and through these early years of training grew the decision that she wanted to be a ballerina.

She arrived in New York in 1942—a long-legged, shy, fifteen-year-old so frightened by the bigness and bustle that she was wildly homesick for Memphis. She started lessons at Ballet Arts, with Agnes de Mille, who, little less than a year later, got her a part in the *corps de ballet* of the musical *Oklahoma!*

Antony Tudor, leading choreographer for Ballet Theatre, saw Diana dance and arranged that she be taken into the company. When sixteen-year-old Diana reported for her first rehearsal, she was overwhelmed with nervousness. Everyone in this strange new company seemed so glamorous and experienced that she felt like the proverbial country cousin. Just when she had become accustomed to the routine of rehearsals and performances, the company

As Eurydice
in Balanchine's
Orpheus

started off on a long tour to the west coast. Now Diana had a new bewildering routine to cope with, living out of suitcases and playing one-night stands in strange cities.

By the next year, Ballet Theatre seemed like home to her. Diana, a sweet, gracious girl, had become one of the favorites of the group and was very much a part of the friendly comradeship and stimulating life. In that year, 1945, she won her first solo role, as Helen in *Helen of Troy.* In her next solo, in Antony Tudor's psychological ballet *Undertow,* she danced for the first time with Hugh Laing. A short while later, when Diana took over the role of one of the Lovers-in-Experience in the melodramatic *Pillar of Fire,* she danced again with Laing. She and her dramatically handsome young partner admired each other instantly as dancers, and that admiration has continued to grow since their marriage in 1947.

They joined the New York City Ballet in 1950, where they continued to dance together, in *Lady of the Camellias* and in *Illuminations*.

On New York City Ballet's lengthy European tour, two years later, Diana gained increasing praise with each new role. When she danced the leads in *Orpheus* and *Symphonie Concertante*, English critics spoke delightedly of her "long and beautiful line," "unmannered style," and "silken movements." When the rest of the cast returned to New York late in 1952, Diana remained in England to work with Gene Kelly on the movie, *Invitation to the Dance*.

The possibility of an accident on stage always lurks in the back of a dancer's mind. An unexpected trapdoor, a too-slippery or uneven floor, a miscalculation of distance—any one of these hazards can cause a dancer to take a spill. Then there are the "near misses" that are invariably the subject of much backstage kidding. Diana's closest miss was the first time she danced as Queen of the Wilis in *Giselle*. Already handicapped by a misty black veil over her face, she was completely blinded when a blue spotlight caught her full in the eyes. Unable to see, she got through the sequence entirely by "feel." Although she was in a panic at the time, she can joke about it now. "Don't ever be a ballet dancer unless you have a sense of humor," she says.

Diana Adams, who has been called the most lyric and poetic of all American dancers, would not be satisfied with any other life than dancing. Though there are no diamonds, and little champagne, she has the greatest reward of all—the knowledge that she is constantly improving as a dancer and is winning increasingly difficult roles and increasingly enthusiastic notices. Much as she enjoys praise from her fellow dancers and the critics, the tribute she cherishes the most is that of her husband Hugh Laing when he says proudly, with his arm about her: "Diana is a perfectly wonderful dancer!"

Alicia Alonso

WHEN little Alicia Martinez joined Cuba's very first ballet class, in Havana some twenty years ago, all the little girls in the class wore tennis shoes, for there was not a pair of ballet slippers in all of Cuba. The class was twittering with excitement the day their teacher held up a pair of pink satin toe-shoes—a gift sent to him from Italy—and announced that they would belong to whichever student they best fitted.

Little Alicia waited with frantic longing until it was her turn to try on the coveted slippers. She slipped her feet into them and, rising on *pointes* at once, *pirouetted* in an ecstasy of pure joy, shouting: "Look, look! They fit!" And so Alicia, that summer of 1932, became the owner of the first toe-shoes in Cuba, an event that has a haunting symbolism, for today she is the first lady of ballet in Cuba. In fact, to the Cuban people, Alicia Martinez—now ballerina Alicia Alonso—is ballet itself.

Petite, fiery Alicia has almost singlehandedly brought ballet to her country, where it was virtually unknown twenty years ago. She is the star of her own company, Ballet Alicia Alonso, which tours from the great coastal cities of Cuba to its tiniest villages. Together with her husband, Fernando Alonso, she directs a flourishing school of ballet, Escuela de Ballet Alicia Alonso, which, though it has been in existence only since 1948, has won the highest award of the Cuban government and a substantial annual subsidy. Students come from all over the island to join her rapidly mushrooming school. "If a youngster is too poor to pay, he comes anyway," says Alicia in her warm, husky voice. "Whether he will be a great dancer or not doesn't matter."

Alicia Martinez inherited from her Spanish forefathers a love of music and rhythm. As a child, she danced from morning till night in the large, busy house in Havana where she was born. Her well-to-do parents belonged to a cultural art center, the Sociedad Pro-Arte, and when it organized Cuba's first ballet class in 1931 little Alicia was enrolled as a matter of course.

From the beginning, Alicia's top position in the class was undisputed. Shortly after she had won the prized toe-shoes, she danced in the first ballet recital ever given by Cuban-trained dancers. She won her first star part when she was twelve, in the *Blue Bird pas de deux*—which had to be rearranged for Alicia to dance alone, because no respectable Cuban family would yet allow their sons to study ballet.

A determined organizer even then, Alicia decided that if she was to be a ballerina, she must find partners. She coaxed her elder brother to bring some of his friends home, promising to teach them wonderful exercises that would make them even better athletes. Her brother finally rounded up a group of slightly doubting young men, among them his best friend—handsome, spirited Fernando Alonso.

The exercises, which began simply to humor the insistent small girl, had an unexpected outcome. Not only did Alicia finally find her partners, but Fernando Alonso decided on a career as a professional ballet dancer—a decision that drew shocked protests from his conservative Cuban family.

Alicia and Fernando practiced daily together, dreaming of the day when they would both be stars. When she was just fifteen, and Fernando twenty-one, they were married, over strenuous objections from Alicia's parents, who felt she was still a child. But the young couple, eager to get started on their careers, knew exactly what they wanted. Fernando led the way. He went to New York, and was accepted by the Mordkin Ballet. Alicia, who had stayed in Cuba to await the birth of their baby, excited at her husband's success, rushed to New York to join him, announcing with determination: "Believe me, as soon as this baby is born, I am going to dance, too!" A month after their little daughter was born, she was dancing—in the same company with Fernando.

The young parents were so full of their new life—baby and ballet all at once—that the days flew by. In addition to nightly

Prima ballerina ALICIA ALONSO in *Don Quixote*

performances at the Mordkin Ballet, they took daily lessons with Mme Alexandra Fedorova, whose studio was the center of ballet activities in New York. The Alonsos made a brief summer tour with Ballet Caravan, and then with several fellow enthusiasts, including Nora Kaye, John Kriza, and Leon Danielian, they joined brand-new Ballet Theatre in 1939.

During the next year and a half, Alicia rose steadily in the company. Her flashing Latin temperament illuminated the ease and fluidity of her movements, her extraordinary *elevation* and her fine classical *line*—all of which marked her as outstanding. The future looked marvelously bright, and already she and Fernando were deep in plans to form their own company in Cuba. Then their little world of youth and gaiety and beauty was shattered overnight.

Alicia suddenly could not see out of her right eye. She went to a doctor, who examined her enormous black eyes carefully, and then said gently: "Go back home to Cuba. You are going to be blind." Alicia would not believe him. Desperately, she consulted another doctor, but his verdict was the same. She had a detached retina, he told her, and the one slim chance of saving her sight was to try a precarious operation. Alicia stoically endured the operation, but it was not a success. The sight in her other eye began to fade, and soon she was completely blind.

Another unsuccessful operation followed. Then came a final operation, after which the doctors told her that she must lie in bed for a full year, with her eyes heavily bandaged and sandbags holding her head motionless. Their orders were severe: "You must not cry, you must not laugh. You must not move at all."

Within her world of darkness, Alicia kept repeating fiercely to herself: "I will stay this year in bed. After that, I am going to get up and dance!" She followed her doctor's orders scrupulously and uncomplainingly, but pleaded that her little daughter not be told that her mother was blind. Every day when the child came into her darkened room, they played a heartbreaking game of "pretend"— that the mother could see her, right through the bandages. So passionately did Alicia pretend that sometimes it seemed as though she really could see the sweet little face so near her own.

Through the endless months she practiced, in her mind, going over each step of each ballet she had ever danced. The long year finally wore away and, when the bandages were removed, Alicia's great dark eyes fluttered open. She could see!

Almost faster than the doctors and her young husband deemed advisable, Alicia began to walk, and then to dance, full of such wild happiness that she could not be held back. She felt she had returned to life. Back with Ballet Theatre in 1945, she began to dance again all the beautiful, familiar roles she had danced in her mind during that endless year of blackness. Then the most coveted role of all, the title role in *Giselle*, was given her. Alonso says today: "It was like a reward—a reward for patience."

Swiftly she rose to stardom. Today, as Ballet Theatre's world-famous *prima ballerina*, she earns vast acclaim for her technical brilliance and sensitive interpretations. She excels in a wide range of roles, from the pure classicism of *Swan Lake* to the stark drama of *Undertow*. In all of them she is called superlative.

Each summer, at the end of the season with Ballet Theatre, she and Fernando return to Cuba, where their dream of a company and a school became a working actuality in 1948. They have seen their school mushroom to an enrollment of three hundred students and become a center for all the arts. They have seen their company, now entirely Cuban-trained, tour with rousing success within their own country and throughout Central and South America. They have seen their own daughter Laurita, now a beautiful teen-aged girl, become a dancer with the Ballet Alicia Alonso.

"Ballet is a hard life," says Alonso, "and if you don't adore it as you do life itself, it can be a bit of torture every day." But it *is* life itself to Alicia Alonso, and the future stretches clear and bright before her. Each winter she will star as guest artist in the ballet capitals of the world, and each summer she will return to her native Cuba, bringing to her school and her company the inspiration of her boundless energies and dynamic talents.

Jean Babilée

IMPULSIVE Jean Babilée, who says he started ballet training "because I wanted to move!" has been in perpetual motion all his life. As a small boy in Paris, where he was born in 1923, Jean was obsessed with the idea of becoming a circus acrobat, and says today with a touch of regret that he could have been a first-class one if he hadn't gone into ballet instead.

When his parents enrolled him at the Opéra Ballet School in Paris, his teachers immediately noted his remarkable agility, but they were frequently baffled by this willful, talented boy who swung so abruptly from furious concentration to almost complete indifference. From the beginning, young Jean himself seemed to know he would be a dancer, but he was often bored with the process of learning.

In the early years of World War II, when he was sixteen, he broke away from the Opéra to put together a small ballet company of his own in Cannes. He danced all the leading roles, was choreographer and director as well, and in the brief months of its existence his little company was a surprising success. When the Germans overran France, he disbanded his company and flung himself into the thick of the resistance movement.

At war's end, Jean Babilée, then twenty-one, returned to Paris and joined Roland Petit's new company, Les Ballets des Champs-Élysées. In the modern, experimental ballets that were this company's specialty, mercurial young Babilée danced better than he had ever danced before. His flair for the dramatic, and his technical brilliance, enhanced the young company's success from the very first.

The year 1946 was a momentous one in Babilée's life. It brought to fulfillment two dreams of long standing: his marriage to serene, blue-eyed Nathalie Philippart, a young dancer with Les

JEAN BABILÉE rehearsing his own ballet *Til Eulenspiegel*

Ballets des Champs-Élysées, and his attainment to a role so magnificently suited to him that it seemed to Babilée to justify his whole existence as a dancer. This role, which brought him instant acclaim, was The Young Man in *Le Jeune Homme et la Mort*.

Babilée himself remembers every vivid detail of that ballet, beginning with the day the company first met on the bare stage with French playwright Jean Cocteau, who had written the macabre story. The dancers listened in a trance as he unfolded his tale of a tortured, despairing young man who destroys his life in the name of his love, who is Death. Rehearsals for this seventeen-minute ballet went on for a full month, sometimes with no music at all, sometimes to swing records picked almost at random. Only at dress rehearsal on the afternoon of the *première* did the astonished dancers hear for the first time the slow, majestic music * that was to form the deliberately shocking contrast to the violent story. Babilée himself was overwhelmed by the emotional experience of dancing out his role of despair and death against this unexpected, magnificent music. He says, shaking his head in wonder: "It was like God looking down on the little people of the world!"

Le Jeune Homme et la Mort was an instant, shattering success. Babilée, as the tormented Young Man, and his wife Nathalie Philippart as Death, gave such powerfully dramatic performances that to see them dance was an emotional experience of startling intensity.

Babilée toured with Les Ballets des Champs-Élysées through Europe, Asia, and South America for five phenomenally successful years. Each ballet he danced brought him increased recognition: *Jeu de Cartes, La Rencontre, La Création, Le Rendezvous*. But he has never surpassed his performance in *Le Jeune Homme et la Mort*. The Young Man is his role, and always will be, no matter who else may dance it.

Les Ballets des Champs-Élysées disbanded in 1950. Babilée, who likes to say he "lacks ambition," promptly flung himself into a whole series of new ventures. He went to the United States, where he appeared for two seasons as guest artist with Ballet

* The Bach Passacaglia in C Minor.

Theatre. He went to Italy as guest artist at the Maggio Musicale in Florence. Back in Paris, he made his own documentary film about backstage ballet life. Under Petit's direction, he danced in six complete ballets for television films, which were released over much of the world in 1953. He made a victorious return to the Paris Opéra in 1953 as choreographer and *premier danseur étoile*—the very highest rank any male dancer can attain.

His eminent position has not changed Jean Babilée, who is an intense individualist, erratic, unpredictable, and often charming. He feigns indifference to his career, saying that although he likes to dance he would really much rather be doing something else. He would rather race his English-built motorcycle, which he claims is the fastest in the world. He would rather indulge his passion for fast automobiles. He would rather go sailing, or fishing, or to a bullfight—anything, he says, that gives him "fun and relief and enjoyment."

One young dancer, who knew him well in the brightest days of Les Ballets des Champs-Élysées, says almost sadly: "Babilée could be the greatest dancer in the world, if only he wanted to be!" But Babilée seems interested only in dancing those roles which please him. What he calls "the old chestnuts" bore him. Although critics often compare his phenomenal dancing in *Afternoon of a Faun* to that of Nijinsky, he shrugs off their comparison impatiently. And although they have called his *Blue Bird pas de deux* magnificent, his own favorite performance of it is the night he leaped, by mistake, right into the audience. "I had an enormous success!" he recalls gleefully.

Jean Babilée is an enigma to the critics. They admit that this ash-blond, brown-eyed young man has "undoubted genius" about him, which makes his dancing, at its best, unequaled. But they bewail the unevenness of his performances, which vary wildly according to how he feels at the moment. Perhaps the most significant comment of all is made by his wife, Nathalie Philippart: "My favorite partner? My husband, Jean Babilée—when he's in a good mood!"

Ruthanna Boris

ALTHOUGH energetic Ruthanna Boris says: "My dreams and ambitions have always been far too many for any one person!" she has made almost a habit of achieving them.

Ruthanna was born in Brooklyn in 1918 of a Russian father and a Viennese mother. Her first remembered ambition was to take ballet lessons. She made her family's life miserable until they finally enrolled her at the Metropolitan Opera Ballet School when she was ten. The coveted lessons seemed slow and dull at first, and she felt with a child's perverseness that she knew more than her teachers. But gradually the impetuous little girl came to accept the importance of the slow, disciplined, traditional training.

At twelve, she was a real member of the *corps de ballet* of the Metropolitan Opera Ballet Company. Four years later, she won her first solo role in the ballet *Reminiscence* with the American Ballet Company.

Ruthanna, whose heart was set on being a classical ballerina, felt she was really on her way. Then, abruptly, one of her teachers at the School of American Ballet told her that she could never become a classical dancer because she was too short and her ankles were too weak. She should concentrate on character roles instead. Completely crushed at first by this verdict, Ruthanna soon decided stubbornly that she *would* be a classical dancer in spite of it. There were other dancers no taller than her 5-feet-1, she told herself fiercely. As for the weak ankles, she set to work immediately on exercises to develop their strength.

She worked for the next two years without any time off, dancing the regular seasons with the American Ballet Company and summers with Ballet Caravan. In 1938 she danced her first ballerina role in the opera *La Gioconda*. Now that her long-sought goal—to become a classical ballerina—was almost within reach,

RUTHANNA BORIS as the Snow Queen in *The Nutcracker*

ambitious Ruthanna promptly set her sights on another—becoming a choreographer.

She had been fascinated watching three young American choreographers (Lew Christensen, William Dollar, and Eugene Loring) at work during her summers with Ballet Caravan, and now began to spend all of her spare time working out dance patterns of her own. Some day, she vowed, her name would be on the program as a choreographer.

Meanwhile, she joined the Ballet Russe de Monte Carlo in 1943 as a soloist, winning praise for her spirited, delightful dancing in the lead roles of *Frankie and Johnny, Serenade,* and *Concerto Barocco.* She rose to ballerina status with her appearance as the Swan Queen in *Swan Lake.*

On September 10, 1947, Ruthanna saw another cherished ambition realized, when the program carried her name as choreographer of *Cirque de Deux.* Critics pronounced her first work "charming," "delightful," and "wittily designed."

Her second ballet, *Quelques Fleurs,* was equally well received, and led to her appointment as choreographer-dancer with the New York City Ballet. Her gay, colorful ballets, *Cakewalk, Kaleidoscope,* and *Will o' the Wisp,* were popular assets to the company's repertoire. In 1951 she began doing choreography for musicals: *Two on the Aisle* and, the following year, *Jollyanna.*

For relaxation after a long working day, tireless Ruthanna and her husband, Frank Hobi (a soloist with the New York City Ballet) like to go dancing or to the theater. They spend many lively evenings with groups of friends in their own apartment, listening to Stan Kenton records, and invariably winding up in spirited discussions of ballet.

Gay, sparkling Ruthanna turns instantly serious when she is talking about her favorite subject—choreography—and of her utopian dream of "millions of well-trained dancers dancing thousands of wonderful new ballets." And at least a few of those "wonderful new ballets," Ruthanna admits with a twinkle in her mischievous brown eyes, she intends to do herself!

Leslie Caron

WHEREVER the movie, *An American in Paris*, was shown, from Hollywood to Hobbs Corners, audiences were bewitched by the provocative dancing and piquant little face of its unknown young French star. American movie-goers felt they personally had discovered this girl, who was part mischievous pixie, part wistful child, and part seductive woman—Leslie Caron.

Actually, she had been "discovered" before, in her own country. As a sixteen-year-old ballerina, she had become the talk of Paris overnight when she starred as the Sphinx in the ballet *La Rencontre.*

Leslie Caron, who was the darling of two continents before she was twenty, was born in Paris on July 1, 1933, the daughter of Claude Çaron, a manufacturing chemist, and Margaret Petit, an American and a former dancer. When the Nazis invaded France, Leslie was taken out of her Paris convent and sent to her grandmother in Cannes. She returned to her Paris home after the liberation of France, fragile and undernourished from the meager wartime diet. Her mother knew that what her daughter needed was plenty of meat, eggs, and milk, but these were hard to get in postwar France. As a last resort, she decided to try ballet lessons to build up Leslie's strength.

Eleven-year-old Leslie was enrolled in the National Conservatory of France, and took to her lessons with the great teacher Volinine, quickly and easily. She was just fourteen when she made her first professional appearance, with Roland Petit's company, dancing a small solo in *The Thirteen Dances.* She was such an appealing performer that Petit promptly took her in as the youngest member of his Ballets des Champs-Élysées in 1948. Leslie loved the small solos she was given, and danced them with sensitivity and flair. David Lichine, guest choreographer with the company, was so taken with the youthful soloist that he picked her for the leading role of the Sphinx in his new ballet *La Rencontre.* On the night of the *première,* the name of sixteen-year-old Leslie Caron was unknown, but the next morning she woke to find herself the most talked-about dancer in Paris. Her picture and story were in all the papers, and night after night people crowded the little Champs-Élysées theater to see for themselves this sphinx-eyed, vibrant young ballerina who had caused such a stir. The American dancer Gene Kelly came to see her one night and was so enchanted by her performance that he went backstage to congratulate her. But Leslie, overcome with shyness, hurried from the theater before he had a chance to meet her.

With the role of the Sphinx, Leslie was firmly established as a ballerina, and shortly set out on a tour of Europe and Egypt with Les Ballets des Champs-Élysées.

In London, she caused another furor in another Lichine ballet, *La Création.* In all the countries they toured, audiences fell under Leslie's spell. At the end of two years, the company returned to Paris to prepare for a tour to South America. Almost on the day of departure, Leslie's parents, feeling that another long tour might prove too much for her frail health, refused to let her go. Leslie was wild with disappointment.

Here fate played a hand. Gene Kelly had returned to Paris especially to find the little ballerina with the wide, tilted blue eyes, whose performance in *La Rencontre* he had never forgotten. He found her and gave her a screen test for the lead in *An American in Paris.* "This was all very fortunate for me," Leslie now says with a wondering shake of her smooth little head.

Hollywood was a new world for this petite French girl, and she found movie-making a frightening ordeal at first. Fortunately, she knew a little English, because her mother had sometimes spoken it at home—"mostly," says Leslie with her impish smile, "when she was scolding me!" But dancing before a camera instead of an audience was very confusing until, she says: "I learned to imagine an audience, and then it was all right."

LESLIE CARON. Above, as the Sphinx in
La Rencontre

One day, while the picture was actually being filmed, Leslie impulsively whacked away at her long dark hair with a pair of nail scissors. When she was through, she had a short, shaggy cut that horrified the MGM directors, but the damage was done. To the studio's surprise, however, her casual gamine haircut set a style all over the country. "But," Leslie says solemnly, "I have had to promise that I will not cut my own hair again!"

Leslie was married to handsome George Hormel, Jr. (heir to the Hormel millions), in Las Vegas in 1951. The young couple moved into a tiny house in Hollywood's Laurel Canyon, where Leslie plays seriously at the new game of housekeeping. She is a familiar sight at the neighborhood supermarket, attired in faded shorts and a cotton shirt. Leslie, who is thrifty in the typical French fashion, cooks and bakes and makes many of her own clothes. Life in the United States is wonderful, this little French girl says enthusiastically. "There is something so optimistic here, especially in California. Maybe it is because of so much sunshine." She loves to bask in the sun, and is never happier than when, as she puts it with her charming accent, she is "planting the yard up."

Hollywood and movie-making became her life. In quick succession she made a series of movies: *The Man with the Cloak*, *Glory Alley*, *The Story of Three Loves*, and *Lili*—with each adding new converts to the Leslie Caron cult.

In spite of her tremendous Hollywood success, she feels a great nostalgia for her days as a ballerina in France. That other life comes back to her as she pores over her scrapbook, which her father started for her in an old account-book. Turning the pages, her eyes go soft with memories and she speaks of her old dancing comrades and of the unforgettable days with Les Ballets des Champs-Élysées.

It may be that some day the memories will crowd too insistently, and ballerina Leslie Caron will be back again—dancing behind the footlights.

Yvette Chauviré

"DANCING is my reason for living, the means of expressing myself and of escaping into a world of the spirit," writes Yvette Chauviré, star of the Paris Opéra, and one of the greatest living classical ballerinas.

Chauviré was born in Paris in 1917 of French parents, her father an industrial engineer and a Sunday painter, and her mother a modiste. "I was ten years old when I entered the school of the Opéra. My mother entered me, knowing that the dance was a part of me, that my wish to dance was as strong as my wish to live."

From the very first, she felt "joy and interest" in her ballet classes, and, as a *petit rat,** soon began to appear in a variety of children's roles in the opera ballets. The child worked daily and devotedly with her teacher at the Opéra, Mlle Couat, a Frenchwoman who taught her the Italian system of ballet.

An imaginative child, little Yvette often was lost in a world of her own fantasies. "I remember when I was thirteen I went to spend my vacation with my grandmother. One day, while she was taking a nap, I slipped out of the house, and went through the fields singing opera tunes. The sun, the bracing air, the big sky inspired me, and I felt marvelous yearnings rising in me. I began to dance, gathering flowers and making up a real ballet. I was aware of nothing around me. I went back home very happy. But the next day, my grandmother overheard two gossips talking in low voices, but not low enough for the sharp ears of my grandmother, and this is what she heard: 'You didn't see? The granddaughter of Mme Chauviré? But that child is insane! Poor little girl, so young, and already crazy!' "

---

* The term "petit rat," which had its origin in a slang phrase, means any young girl beginner at the Opéra School who dances minor roles in the opera ballets. Many of today's leading French ballerinas began as *rats* at the Opéra—Colette Marchand, Renée Jeanmaire, Nina Vyroubova, among others.

At thirteen, she graduated from the class of *petits rats* and into the Opéra's "first class." From then on, she progressed slowly from one rank to the next, dancing her first important solos when she became a *grand sujet* at eighteen.

She passed the examination for *première danseuse* (a rank equivalent to that of ballerina) in December 1936, when she was nineteen. Now came her first major role, when she took over in Lifar's ballet *David Triomphant*. Very shortly afterwards this young dancer won two other major roles: Queen of the Wilis in *Giselle* and the leading role in *Prométhée*, opposite Lifar himself. "It was a great honor for me to dance with Lifar, a marvelous stimulant and a mad responsibility!" she says, because Serge Lifar, ballet master and choreographer of the Opéra, has been her greatest inspiration all through her career. Referring to him as "the master," she says he inspired all the dancers at the Opéra "because he is himself inspired and burns with a creative flame."

Chauviré's first nine years of training had been in the Italian system of ballet technique; a year after she became a *première danseuse* she decided she must learn the equally important Russian system. She worked with Boris Kniaseff, an eminent Russian teacher in Paris, for three intensive years. Critics say she owes much of the perfection of her classic technique to this remarkable teacher.

Early in 1945, Chauviré scored such a triumph in Lifar's ballet *Istar* that she was elevated to the top position at the Opéra—*première danseuse étoile*. Having attained this pinnacle at the age of twenty-seven, and already possessed of an almost perfect technique, she decided that the time had come for her to work alone— "to assert my own personality and get away from influences, either Italian or Russian."

"I studied my body constantly in front of the mirror, demanding the impossible of myself—weeping, suffering, but dancing, alive and vibrant—singing with all my body. This laboratory work of mine went on for four years, and was very thrilling to me." And during this entire period, everything she learned in her hours of

YVETTE CHAUVIRÉ. Above, in *Le Cygne*

solitary work was reflected in the ever increasing brilliance of her performances at the Opéra.

Chauviré made her first lengthy tour outside France when she joined the Nouveau Ballet de Monte Carlo in 1946 and toured with them to Italy and England. Her dancing was greeted rapturously in both countries by audiences and critics. British critic Arnold Haskell wrote: "Yvette Chauviré's *Giselle* is the greatest and most moving I have seen since Pavlova. It is a model for every dancer of this generation, an inspiring model devoid of the slightest mannerism." This role is Chauviré's own favorite "because it is at the same time real and unreal. Because it demands technique, poetry, lightness, emotion, personality—expression of body and soul."

She returned to the Opéra after this short tour, where she starred for the next two years. Early in 1949, she again appeared as guest artist throughout Europe, and made her first appearance in the United States * as guest artist with the Ballet Russe de Monte Carlo. American audiences found her an enchanting dancer, and particularly admired her *Giselle, Swan Lake,* and her own choreography of *Romeo and Juliet,* in which Oleg Tupine was her partner.

Her American debut was followed by appearances with Dolin's Festival Ballet in England, a return engagement to Milan, and a triumphant five-month return tour to America. Of this tour, Chauviré says simply: "I was satisfied with our success. Americans adore the dance."

Chauviré lives a carefully planned life in which everything is weighed for its effect on her dancing. She takes a daily class at eleven, a private lesson after lunch (when she does not have a rehearsal) followed by two hours at home, having a massage, attending to mail, and resting. If she is not performing, she goes to bed early with a book, or goes to the theater or a "good film."

When she has an evening performance, she arrives at the

* She had already made a film appearance in *La Mort du Cygne,* released in America as *Ballerina.*

theater precisely three hours before curtain time, and receives no one but her husband, Constantin Nepo. "I like to be alone, to study myself before the mirror. I may sing a little, to make sure of the expression of my make-up. I pay particular attention to my eyes. I usually arrange my hair myself. I go on to exercises. At the half-hour call, warmly dressed, I try the difficult passages. I check my ballet slippers constantly, and can never make up my mind which ones to choose. Then the bell! I feel nervous, and I glance at my good luck charms and a dear photo. After several seconds of con-centration, I am anxious to be on stage, to feel the floor once more before the performance. My emotion and my feelings of responsi-bility are strong. After a performance, I never feel entirely satisfied, for the ideal is rarely attained. Many times I return crying to my dressing room—the applause of the public and the compliments of my friends are not always a consolation."

She is careful not to accept too many social invitations, saying wisely: "Well-known dancers are always feted, but a dancer's life allows very little leisure, and one must spare oneself as much as possible. After all, an artist's name is made on the stage, and not in the drawing-room!"

The greatest joy she finds outside of dancing is in painting. She is an accomplished artist and is married to an artist—Count Constantin Nepokoitchitsky—who paints under the name of Constantin Nepo. One of Chauviré's favorite pastimes is posing for her husband who, besides designing costumes and stage sets for ballet, is a portrait painter.

What does she ask of the future? "To continue to progress towards my ideal. Then to teach, giving everything I have ac-quired." In the meanwhile, Yvette Chauviré, dancing in *Les Mi-rages, Le Roi Nu, Alexandre le Grand,* and in the classics for which she is rightly famed, serves as an inspiration to the younger dancers at the Paris Opéra, and to the audiences of the world.

Yvonne Chouteau

YVONNE CHOUTEAU, in spite of her name, couldn't be more American. The pride of Oklahoma, she is one of a long line of Chouteaus prominent in that state's history. There was Jean Pierre Chouteau, who in 1771 became the first white settler in what is now Oklahoma. There was Yvonne's great-great-grandmother, who was a Shawnee Indian princess. There is Yvonne herself—a vividly attractive girl with strawberry-blonde hair, sun-tanned skin, and a warm, friendly grin—who is the youngest ballerina with the Ballet Russe de Monte Carlo, and the only member of Oklahoma's State Hall of Fame under fifty years of age!

Her state likes to gloss over the fact that Yvonne was actually born in Texas, while her parents were hurrying home to Oklahoma to await her birth. But ever since that first unscheduled appearance in 1929, Yvonne has played the part of native daughter to the hilt. When she was just four, she danced a little Indian ceremonial dance, in full feathered regalia, as Oklahoma's official representative at the Chicago Century of Progress. From then on, her lively little figure began to be a familiar sight at state occasions throughout Oklahoma. She was the much-publicized heroine of all these occasions, and columns of newspaper space were devoted to her every appearance.

Her family, eager for their talented daughter to have the best teachers, took her to California when she was eight, to study with Ernest Belcher and Adolph Bolm. Three years later, she applied for a scholarship at the School of American Ballet, and won it over competition from every part of the country.

After three work-filled years, Yvonne auditioned for the Ballet Russe de Monte Carlo, when she was fourteen, and was accepted —the youngest American-born dancer ever to become a member of that company. The company's prima ballerina, Alexandra Dani-

YVONNE CHOUTEAU in *Gaité Parisienne*

lova, took an instant interest in this sprightly youngster, and
Yvonne, who had long idolized her, was overjoyed and awed at
being singled out as her protégée. Under Danilova's careful tute-
lage, she danced her first solo when she was only fifteen, as Prayer
in *Coppélia*, a role that Danilova selected because it had been her
own first solo.

She celebrated her sixteenth birthday dancing her next solo in
Le Beau Danube, opposite the great Massine. Critics acclaimed
her performance as delightful and appealing. It was a perfect
birthday.

For the next five years, Yvonne toured with the Ballet de
Monte Carlo, adding experience and polish with each new role.
She won her first ballerina role in 1950, as Juliet in *Romeo and
Juliet,* which seemed the fulfillment of all this young girl's dreams.
"I'm mad for Shakespeare anyway," she says with a sigh.

Yvonne is an earnest, enthusiastic youngster, intensely ideal-istic about her career as a dancer. She works the year round, driven by a persistent desire for improvement. She spends her summers, between seasons, studying in New York, preferably with her cur-rent idol, choreographer Antony Tudor, whose modern ballets seem perfection to her.

She has brief moods occasionally, when a dancer's life doesn't seem worth the effort. She contemplates wistfully the things that are taboo for a ballet dancer. She must pass up the gooey ice-cream sundaes she loves, in order to keep her figure slim and supple. "I get sort of tired of steaks," she says pensively. She must avoid both horseback riding and tennis (though she is accomplished at both) because they are bad for her dancing muscles. Though she may swim—and does, enthusiastically—she must be careful of sunburn and overexertion. She mustn't stay out too late at parties. She must remember every minute of every day that she has a performance at eight-thirty that night.

Sometimes, after a particularly rigorous season, all of these restrictions seem unbearable to Yvonne. More than once, she has thrown up her hands and announced flatly: "I'm *not* coming back next season!" With a defiant toss of her blonde mane, she packs her bags and heads for the nearest seashore. She's going to do exactly what she wants for a whole, lazy summer: swim, play tennis, ride horseback, get sunburned, and gorge on double chocolate sundaes!

Somehow, though, the carefree days begin to pall. She opens each morning's mail with increasing eagerness to hear what is going on with her ballet friends. A note from her good friend Leon Danielian tells of a new role he is rehearsing. A letter from another friend describes a new ballet going into production. Suddenly the seashore is a meaningless place, and back she flies to New York, eagerly picking up the threads that bind her to ballet.

"Dancing is something that I simply cannot live without," Yvonne Chouteau says, and then adds hastily, before anyone can smile at her youthful earnestness: "That may sound corny, but it's *true!*"

Leon Danielian

LEON DANIELIAN is an energetic, talkative young man whose genuine liking for people is so strong that it has led him to remark: "If I have a hobby, I guess you could call it making friends." He has made so many friends, in the various places all over the world where his life as a *premier danseur* has taken him, that he is likely to run into someone he knows in the unlikeliest corners of the earth. Even on a recent tour to Africa, where Leon had never been before, he bumped into acquaintances in both Algiers and Casablanca. His habit of collecting people has become almost a standing joke with his associates, who kid him good-naturedly about it.

Likable Leon Danielian talks incessantly—and amusingly—his long, mobile face alight, and his nervous body in constant motion. "It is impossible to shut me up," he says with disarming candor, and adds that if there is anyone more talkative than an Armenian, it is another Armenian. This love of talk, Leon says, he inherited from his Armenian parents, along with his snapping black eyes and crisp dark hair.

He insists that he has no "life story." With his characteristic grin, he says that he is just an ordinary guy with an unglamorous past. "I am sorry to say that I didn't escape from Russia in a boxcar, and wasn't a prodigy at three—nothing dramatic at all."

Born in New York in 1920, Leon began his dancing lessons under protest. His mother insisted that seven-year-old Leon and his younger sister go to a ballet class that a friend of hers was starting in the local Armenian church. Leon, who claims he was shy in those days, was painfully self-conscious when he found himself performing at the *barre*. He dreaded the lessons, but there was no escape.

As his first awkwardness wore off, Leon began to take pleasure in the fact that he could do the exercises with the greatest of ease. When the teacher had taught him all she could, she strongly advised Leon's parents to send him to her own former teacher, Mikhail Mordkin. Proud as they were of their talented son, they could not afford the tuition; but Leon auditioned at the Mordkin School anyway and won a scholarship.

Young Leon was enormously stimulated by his new classes, even though he had never seen a ballet performance, and had only the vaguest idea of what he was working toward. Then, one unforgettable day in 1935, he was picked as an extra for a performance of *Scheherazade.* Fifteen-year-old Leon was confused and awed as he stood in the wings on the night of the performance, all made up and ready for his part. On stage, *Firebird,* the ballet that preceded *Scheherazade* on the program, was in full swing. Leon, trying to keep out of the stagehands' way, craned his neck to catch glimpses of the famous dancers, Alexandra Danilova and Leonide Massine, who were dancing the lead roles. Almost hypnotized, he watched them whirling in the blinding red spotlights, and listened to the staccato beat of Danilova's hard-toed slippers. Leon stood spellbound as Danilova and Massine took their curtain calls. In a never-to-be-forgotten moment, everything that he had learned suddenly crystallized. "So this is what it is really like!" he remembers saying to himself. "This is ballet!"

From then on, nothing could stop young Danielian. When his teacher, Mikhail Mordkin, formed his new company in 1937, Leon was asked to join as a member of the *corps de ballet.* Two years later, along with some of the other Mordkin dancers, he became a part of another brand-new company, Ballet Theatre. It was in the Original Ballet Russe, which he joined in 1941, that the increasing sureness and fire of his dancing began to attract real attention. When he moved on, two years later, to the Ballet Russe de Monte Carlo, he quickly leaped to the rank of *premier danseur.* Today he is the top dancer with this same company, and one of its biggest drawing-cards.

One of Danielian's happiest experiences was dancing as guest

LEON DANIELIAN in *Impromptu au Bois* with Les Ballets des Champs-Élysées

artist with Les Ballets des Champs-Élysées. He danced in France for a season and then went with them for a tour of Africa in 1950. This was high adventure for travel-loving Leon Danielian, who was fascinated by Africa—especially by its strange, veiled women, who, he says, seemed to him the most exotic in the world.

The vitality and zest for living which are the key to Danielian, the man, are also the key to Danielian, *premier danseur*. His dancing is vigorous and dramatic, and he carries his compact body with a proud assurance that comes from knowing he is master of his trade. He dances all the ballets in the repertoire of the Ballet Russe de Monte Carlo, and is superb in such works as *Le Beau Danube*, *Afternoon of a Faun*, and the *Pas de Deux Classique*. But he prefers the roles that let him indulge his innate love of comedy—especially the Peruvian in *Gaité Parisienne*, which is a delight to him because it enables him to use his flair for characterization and mimicry. He has no favorite roles—he dances them all so often that any possible favorite soon loses its sparkle—"rather like having champagne every night," he says.

Every time he dances a new role, he is so wrapped in concentration that he finds himself quite hazy about the actual performance. "The curtain goes up, the curtain goes down, and I say to myself: 'My goodness, did I do that?'" Opening nights are the same. He is oblivious of everything—how many curtain calls he took, how he got on or off stage, or with whom he talked in the wings. If someone asks him for an autograph while he is still in this after-performance daze, he has even been known to forget his own name.

When the performance is over, Leon is so keyed up that he has to let off steam. He always arranges to go out with a group of friends for a midnight snack. He says: "I never eat alone if I can help it." But the food is secondary to the talk. In any gathering, Leon is the life of the party, with his fund of anecdotes and his amusing backstage gossip. He will talk all night about ballet, and the people in it, because, next to his career, people are the most engrossing interest in Leon Danielian's life.

Alexandra Danilova

THE performance that night at the San Francisco Opera House had long since ended, but the audience refused to leave the theater. Standing up, they kept up a steady, rolling barrage of applause until at last the massive gold curtains parted once more— for the final curtain call. The spotlights focused on a small, radiant figure standing alone on the vast stage, surrounded by heaped masses of flowers. At sight of her, the audience burst into a renewed frenzy of applause. She stretched out her arms in an appealing gesture of gratitude and love, with her great gray eyes overflowing with tears. There were tears in many other eyes that night, because this performance in 1951 was rumored to be the farewell appearance in San Francisco of Alexandra Danilova, *prima ballerina assoluta.*

All over the Western world, ballet-goers felt this same nostalgic emotion at the rumor of Danilova's retirement. For more than twenty years, she had dominated the ballet scene, and her magnetic personality and superb artistry had become a living legend. Her retirement would mark the end of a fabulous era. To her worldwide public, who felt sentimental about her, it would also be a uniquely personal loss.

As it turned out, this was not the end. Danilova made a determined effort to retire. She joined the teaching staff of a ballet school in Dallas, and for a few months devoted herself wholeheartedly to her young students. But when Mia Slavenska and Frederic Franklin formed a new ballet company in 1952 and begged her to come with them as guest artist, Danilova promptly and delightedly left for New York. Back once more in the life she has loved so long, she says now that all she wants is to "continue dancing all over the world with different companies as guest artist." In the still indefinite future, when she will retire, then she will "teach and help others to become dancers."

Alexandra Danilova is the last of the great Russian ballerinas now dancing in the Western world. In her is carried on the noble tradition of the Imperial School of Ballet in St. Petersburg—a school whose training has never been equaled by any other, anywhere. The most famous dancers the world has ever known have been products of this school—among them Nijinsky, Pavlova, and Karsavina.

Danilova was born in Peterhov, Russia. Before she was four, both of her parents died, and the little girl was handed about from grandmother to godmother to aunt, and finally adopted by Mme Lydia Gotovzeva, a woman of considerable wealth and social standing. Little Alexandra, who was always called by the pet name of Choura, was a lively, friendly child whose irrepressible spirits were apparently undaunted by her unsettled early years. Her new aunt doted on her, and little Choura was full of delight at her luxurious new home.

She spent many hours dancing before the full-length mirror in her lavish nursery. One day her aunt, passing by the door, watched in amazement as the little girl rose effortlessly to the very points of her toes. "At once," says Danilova now with a flash of her characteristic humor, "my aunt think I am second Pavlova, and she decide to send me to Theater School."

On the eventful day that Choura, accompanied by her aunt, presented herself at the Imperial School of Ballet in St. Petersburg, she was upset to see a tremendous crowd of other children already waiting for auditions. She knew that only a handful would be chosen. But little Choura—a doll-like creature with long chestnut hair, huge gray eyes and sparkling charm—got through the long day of examinations with unruffled poise. One by one the original group of 350 was whittled down, and at length Choura happily learned that she—the tiniest and youngest (eight and a half) of the group—was one of eighteen who had been chosen.

From the very first day, the children were expected to fit into a rigid pattern of discipline and intensive work. Choura, however, flitted unconcernedly through her schedule, which began with classes every morning at nine and continued until bedtime at nine

ALEXANDRA DANILOVA as the Snow Queen in *The Nutcracker*

each night. Finally she was told that she would be expelled if she did not mend her ways. "They give me one more year to improve," she says now with a twinkle, "and I make myself concentrate immediately!" Once she had made up her mind, she not only accepted the School's demands cheerfully, but did far more than was asked of her. At the end of her second year, lively little Choura passed at the head of her class.

Now her progress began in earnest. In addition to her strenuous lessons at the School, she began to appear with other children in occasional opera ballets at the famous Maryinsky Theatre. Choura, who was always placed in the front row of the dancers because she was so tiny, could watch every move of the great artists who appeared on stage. By studying them, both in rehearsal and in performance, and by taking part in professional productions herself, little Choura absorbed much of the beauty and tradition for which the Maryinsky had long been famous.

When the Revolution burst over Russia in 1917, there was little outward effect on the life of the students at first, for their school routine went on unchanged. But gradually they began to suffer, as food became more and more scarce, and there was less and less fuel. Choura, with never quite enough to eat, often shivered with cold as she kept up her demanding schedule at the School and at the Theatre. The years that followed were difficult ones, full of increasing work and privations. After nine long years, the day came when little Choura and four other girls—all who remained of the original eighteen—were graduated from the School. Overnight the student Choura Danilova was transformed into Mlle Alexandra Danilova, ballet dancer.

As a certified professional, she was automatically taken into the Russian State Ballet. In its *corps de ballet* of 250 dancers, Choura again had a front-row position, partly because she was still tiny, and partly because her charm and technique were even then outstanding. When at last she began to grow, and reached her full height of 5-feet-4, the front-rank spot was hers on merit alone.

She broke from the ranks of *corps de ballet* for the first time as

Prayer in *Coppélia.* Even today Danilova laughingly insists that she got this role (which calls for the dancer's hair to hang loose down her back) not because of her dancing but because of her long wavy chestnut hair!

Although the young Danilova gained increasing notice as a dancer, the privations of her personal life went on unchanged in the chaos of post-revolutionary Russia. Wistfully she dreamed of life in other countries—where food was plentiful, and everyone had beautiful new clothes. She often spoke of her dreams to a rising young choreographer in the company, Gheorghi Balanchivadze, who has today achieved international fame as George Balanchine. It was he who persuaded Choura to take a gamble with him, joining a small group of dancers who were going to try their luck in Western Europe. Danilova left Russia with the little band one wintry day in 1924, bubbling over with anticipation and never dreaming that she was leaving her native country forever.

The unheralded little troupe, calling itself The Russian State Dancers, made its way slowly through Germany and England, and landed in London almost completely broke. Choura, in the midst of the plentiful food and beautiful clothes of which she had long dreamed, could not enjoy them, for she was penniless. She was desperately homesick as well, because she had just learned that her period of leave from Russia had expired. She was an exile from home forever.

Later in Paris, when things looked most bleak, Serge Diaghilev, director of the most famous ballet company in the world, heard of the stranded Russian dancers, and sent for them. After watching them dance, he took the whole troupe into his renowned company, the Diaghilev Ballets Russes. Choura, who had been a lost little stranger, began to feel more at home when she found herself surrounded by her own countrymen in this company. She worshipped Diaghilev from the first, and found that under his inspired direction she was dancing better than she had ever danced before.

Choura started out as a soloist. But after her first season, the company's *prima ballerina* failed to return from vacation, and

Choura was allowed to take over for her. Desperately she worked to justify Diaghilev's faith in her, rehearsing the roles which were soon to bring her fame: leading parts in *Swan Lake, Les Sylphides, Carnaval,* and *Firebird.* In 1927 the title of ballerina was officially hers.

When her fame as a ballerina began to grow, Choura felt humbly that she owed everything to Diaghilev, and that her whole future as a dancer lay in his guiding hands. Then, after a particularly triumphant season in 1929, during which Choura first began to feel a sense of confidence in her own ability, she heard the staggering news—Serge Diaghilev was dead!

Danilova was stunned with grief. It was an overwhelming personal loss for her, because she felt that without him her career was ended. His death marked the end of the entire company, and the dancers scattered throughout Europe in small disorganized groups.

It was during this period of uncertainty that Choura married an Italian engineer, Giuseppe Massera. Her happiness with him was short-lived, for he died four years later.

Danilova, deeply depressed by this latest tragedy, welcomed the invitation of Col. de Basil to join his young company in 1933. Although his Ballet Russe, with its three Original Baby Ballerinas, had won considerable fame, De Basil felt that the company needed one outstanding, experienced ballerina at its head. He brought Danilova in as *prima ballerina.* She toured with De Basil's company for five years in both Europe and the United States, and was greeted everywhere with increasingly wild acclaim.

Audiences idolized her, and crowds waited at the stage door after every performance to catch a glimpse of this chic, magnetic figure whose dancing was already a legend. With the Ballet Russe de Monte Carlo from 1938 to 1951, she continued her conquest of Europe, South America, and the United States, each year adding new laurels to her already heavy crown.

Critics, who hailed her dancing as perfection itself, were astounded when she grew steadily and perceptibly more magnificent with each passing season. "Perfection piled on perfection!" they wrote in wonder, and bestowed on Alexandra Danilova the supreme title of *prima ballerina assoluta*.

What has made Alexandra Danilova so great? There are many answers to that question—but no complete answer. She has a perfectly controlled, marvelously proportioned body, and a flawless technique built on years of incomparable training. She has a wide artistic range which allows her to dance everything from great classical ballets to purely national and character dances with equal effect. She has a personal magnetism and a vivid individuality which fill every corner of the theater. She is always Danilova, whether as the Swan Queen in *Swan Lake* or the Glove Seller in *Gaité Parisienne*. It is the combination of all these qualities, plus the indefinable aura of greatness itself, that audiences crowd to see.

Ballet-goers and critics alike pay homage to Alexandra Danilova—one of the greatest ballerinas of all time. Just as significant a tribute is the loving affection with which her fellow dancers everywhere speak of her. "Ah, little Choura!" they say with a fond smile. "There is no one like her in all the world!"

Anton Dolin

IN SUSSEX, England, a son born to an English sportsman and an Irish writer in 1904 was christened with the elegant name of Sydney Francis Patrick Chippendall Healey-Kay. As a boy he was called Patrick, but when he got his first dancing job he adopted the name that was to bring him world acclaim—Anton Dolin. This name is inescapably linked with a long-vanished era in ballet, which has never been surpassed for elegance and glory—the days of Serge Diaghilev. Anton Dolin is one of the few remaining dancers who was molded and polished by the great impresario himself. As *premier danseur* during those "red plush" days of the Ballets Russes, Dolin acquired a background of splendor and tradition such as no younger *premier danseur* today can claim.

Pat Healey-Kay was nine years old when he began ballet lessons at a little school in Brighton. He rapidly outgrew that first school, and went to London to study with Mme Seraphima Astafieva, the first Russian dancer to open a school where English youngsters could learn the Russian system of ballet. Young Pat was fascinated by these lessons at once, and wanted to shine in the eyes of his teacher, whom he adored. She called him her little "Patté," and told him over and over that he should "work hard and improve, improve, and then improve." Madame's most promising pupils were the ones who got the most raps on their legs from her cane—her way of pointing out mistakes. As his mother said: "Pat must have pleased her greatly, because his legs were always black and blue!"

He had been at her school for several years when one day a scrawny, dark-haired little girl arrived for her first lesson. This was Pat's first meeting with the girl who was to become his most famous partner—Alicia Markova.

When he was in his early teens, Pat began to appear in Lon-

ANTON DOLIN

don amateur dancing festivals and theatricals. His early taste of applause made the handsome, dark-haired boy more than ever impatient for the life of a real professional. The one ballet company in all the world he had set his sights on joining was the Diaghilev Ballets Russes.

As soon as the posters went up announcing the 1921 London season of the Ballets Russes, seventeen-year-old Pat, bearing his new name of Anton Dolin, applied for an audition. Diaghilev took him in as a provisional member of his *corps de ballet* for that season. Young English Dolin was the only non-Russian in that whole galaxy of glittering Russian-born stars, which included such great names as Pierre Vladimiroff, Vera Trefilova, Olga Spessivtzeva, and Lubov Egorova. Nothing in his eventful life since has ever erased Dolin's awed impressions of that season at London's famous Alhambra Theatre. One of his first appearances was in the full-length production of *Sleeping Beauty,* in which the Russian-trained dancers were so dazzling that he recalls it as "the greatest production of a classical ballet that I have ever seen."

When the season was over, Dolin went back to Mme Asta-fieva, where he worked with renewed frenzy to improve enough so that he would be taken into Diaghilev's company as a regular member. So well did he succeed that two years later Diaghilev took him on as a soloist.

Now began the most intensive work that young Dolin had ever known. He was under the constantly critical eye of Serge Diaghilev and of ballet mistress Bronislava Nijinska, both of whom demanded nothing less than perfection. Another promising young dancer, the Russian refugee Serge Lifar, was added to the company's ranks, and Dolin, immediately sensing a rival, worked harder than ever to keep his own position. Diaghilev, who instinctively knew that these two young men were the great *premier danseurs* of the future, drove them unceasingly. He carefully supervised the training of each of them, and had the famous teacher, Enrico Cecchetti, brought in largely for their benefit.

Finally, when Dolin was nineteen, Diaghilev allowed him to

dance the lead role of Daphnis in *Daphnis and Chloë*. Immediately after each performance, Diaghilev sent for the perspiring young dancer and pointed out in critical detail each place where his performance had been lacking. Seldom was there a word of praise. But any notice from the great man, Dolin knew, was a mark of favor.

Dolin lost his status as the only non-Russian member of the company when, in 1923, the English soloist Ninette de Valois (who was later the founder of the Sadler's Wells Ballet) joined the Ballets Russes. They became instant allies, united by their common desire to see the English recognized as dancers. Then the third English recruit was added to this fast-mushrooming company—the girl whom Dolin had first met at ballet school, Alicia Markova, now fourteen and a dancer of great promise.

Dolin was now beginning to stand out in the company. He not only shared in the worldwide success of the Ballets Russes, but won acclaim for himself. Some of his most brilliant successes were danced with the sparkling and gifted Alexandra Danilova. She still delights in teasing him with a remark she claims he made immediately after their performance together in the *Blue Bird pas de deux*. Danilova smilingly admits she was overweight at the time, and Dolin, after hoisting her through the *pas de deux*'s many lifts, stamped off stage in exasperation, fuming: "I am a dancer, *not* a porter!" Danilova always concludes this story with a gay laugh and the statement that she began dieting that very night.

The name of Anton Dolin blazed across the world of ballet in June of 1924, with the *première* of *Le Train Bleu* in Paris. This ballet had been created especially to show off his versatile talents, and was important as the first of a completely new type of ballet— the forerunner of such modern ballets as *Fancy Free* and *Interplay*. *Le Train Bleu* was a satire on the overblown athletes who frequented the Riviera—the golf, swimming, and tennis champions. Anton Dolin, himself an accomplished sportsman, brought to this role a devastating humor and a display of acrobatic prowess which made him the sensation of that unforgettable season.

Five years later, in August 1929, Dolin's own world of ballet collapsed, with the tragic death of Diaghilev. Dolin, distressed at the plight of the company's dancers, who didn't know where to turn, soon began to cast about for a way to pull together some of the fragments of the now-dead Ballets Russes. In 1930, with his friend De Valois, he was instrumental in founding the Camargo Society in London, where many of the dancers found haven. As *premier danseur,* Dolin danced in this predominantly English company with two of the former Ballets Russes' stars: Olga Spessivtzeva and Alicia Markova.

Then began a series of ballet associations in which Anton Dolin made ballet history: as *premier danseur* with the old Vic-Wells Ballet (now famous as the Sadler's Wells Ballet); as partner and director of the famous Markova-Dolin Ballet, which toured in Europe from 1935 to 1937; as guest artist with the De Basil Ballet Russe de Monte Carlo on its Australian tour. He joined Ballet Theatre at its inception in 1939 as *premier danseur* and choreographer. Here, in addition to memorable revivals of *Swan Lake, Giselle,* and *Princess Aurora,* he also did choreography for new ballets: *Quintet, Capriccio, Romantic Age,* and *Pas de Quatre,* which the critics called a real masterpiece.

After eight years with Ballet Theatre, his old friend De Valois begged him to return to England as guest artist with Sadler's Wells Ballet. Since 1950, he has been *premier danseur,* choreographer, and artistic director of his Festival Ballet, for a time the resident company of Monte Carlo—now seen throughout much of Europe. The perfection and polish of the dancers in his company are a reflection of Dolin's own incomparable training and artistic maturity. When Markova danced a season with him, Dolin's partnership of her was called "one of the miracles of contemporary ballet."

Anton Dolin is a giant in the world of ballet, but it is his warm, human qualities that make him extraordinary as an individual as well. He has an irresistible love of people, and an incurable fondness for talk—for which he is almost apologetic, but which his friends relish. He is still an ardent sportsman—as much at home on water skis as in ballet slippers. He recently had to give up tennis, he says ruefully, because it was getting a little too strenuous. He readily admits to his little whims and foibles: he hates to travel by boat or automobile, and will go to almost any lengths to avoid them; he loves to gamble in a small way at *chemin de fer*. He confesses that before a performance he still suffers from nerves, which he tries to allay with a little ritual that never varies: "A very silent prayer, a sign of the cross, and plenty of rosin on the soles of my shoes."

His love of talk and his easy flow of words has spilled over into writing. Among his books are a delightfully chatty autobiography, *Ballet Go Round*, an equally informal biography of his friend Alicia Markova, and a little gem of ballet technique, *The Art of Partnering*. This art, of which he writes so knowledgeably, is almost a lost art today, when the average young *premier danseur* is more intent on showing himself off than in showing off his partner. No higher tribute could be paid to Dolin, on this score, than that of Arnold Haskell: "Anton Dolin is the last great *premier danseur* who understands, as in the old tradition, the truly great art of partnering."

André Eglevsky

ANDRÉ EGLEVSKY's life, reduced to capsule form, follows the almost classic pattern that people associate with famous ballet dancers: the flight from the Russian Revolution, the childhood as an emigrant in Paris, the lessons begun because of ill health, the impressive list of associations with ballet companies long since disbanded and partners long since retired, and even the inevitable plan for the future after dancing—to open a ballet school.

When he joined the vital young New York City Ballet in 1951, veteran performer André Eglevsky was just as dazzling as when Europe first admired his dancing fireworks at Monte Carlo in the early thirties. Audiences gasped, as they always have, at his great leaps, in which he hangs in mid-air for an unbelievable moment. They were agape both at the speed of his smooth, flashing *pirouettes* and at the incredible slowness of his elegant *turns*. Eglevsky runs through these technical feats with the ease and nonchalance of a magician running through his bag of tricks. His unfailing showmanship led one critic to call him "a monument of dancing mechanism."

He is impressive the minute he steps on the stage. He has a handsome face, with heavy-winged eyebrows, deeply set gray-green eyes, and a strongly chiseled nose. He has a virile physique, and his body is so beautifully proportioned that he looks even taller than his 5-feet-10.

Eglevsky, an American citizen since 1939, lives a domestic suburban life that is unusual for a dancer of such eminence. He believes that "a normal life is better for a dancer," and for that reason endures a tedious daily trip from New York City to his home in Massapequa, Long Island. Except when he is on tour, he spends all of his time there with his family: his wife, the former dancer Leda Anchutina, and their three children—André, Jr., Paul,

ANDRÉ EGLEVSKY in *A La Françaix*

and little Maria. He enjoys puttering around the house doing odd jobs and working on his hobbies of stamp collecting, leatherwork, and his extensive collection of antique carpentry tools. He also enjoys taking backstage movies at the ballet, and going fishing.

This life of his, which runs so smoothly now, began in Moscow, where he was born during the first tumultuous year of the Revolution. His father, a Cossack officer, narrowly escaped, and with his family made his difficult way to Paris, which had become the mecca for hordes of refugees. Here André grew up. And here his father, in order to support his family, became a chef—a profession that he still follows in the United States today.

By the time he was eight, André, a tall, spindly lad, had suffered one serious illness after another. His worried mother, knowing what miracles the disciplined exercises of ballet training can often accomplish, enrolled him in ballet class. André was rebellious at first, but when he began to notice that he was actually developing muscles from doing the exercises, he wouldn't have given them up for anything. His lessons finally became so important that he could think of nothing but becoming a ballet dancer. His mother, seeing how earnest he was, and how strong and healthy he had become, took him to study with the eminent teacher, Volinine, when he was thirteen.

Just a year later, he joined the *corps de ballet* of Col. de Basil's Ballet Russe—where he attracted a good deal of attention both for his good looks and for his very noticeable ability as a dancer. In only six months he was dancing leading roles: *Les Sylphides, Swan Lake.* In *Les Présages*, where he partnered the famous star Danilova, he showed such mature assurance that audiences were astonished to learn that he was just sixteen.

In the four years he danced with Ballet Russe, Eglevsky made quite a name for himself as a *premier danseur*. In 1935, he joined Leon Woicikowski's ballet, and a year later the René Blum Ballet. Although he learned much as an artist from his association with these companies, he was filled with a mounting sense of frustration. Discouraged by the low salary scale (of which all dancers complained) and the interminable clashes of temperament between dancers and directors, he resigned from the René Blum company and came to America in 1937 to try something different.

He danced in Radio City Music Hall for a while, and had a fling at musical comedy in *Great Lady*. But the financial insecurity of these hit-and-miss engagements was even worse than he had known before. Soon he was back in ballet again, as *premier danseur* with the American Ballet Company, dancing at the Metropolitan Opera House. It was there that he met Leda Anchutina, a dancer with the same company. They were married in 1938.

During the next fourteen years, Eglevsky danced as *premier danseur* with almost every important ballet company: Ballet Russe de Monte Carlo, Ballet Theatre, Original Ballet Russe, De Cuevas Grand Ballet. He joined the New York City Ballet in 1951. During these years he became famous the world over as a classical *premier danseur*. His astonishing virtuosity was particularly apparent in such roles as Apollo in *Apollon Musagète*, the Prince in *The Nutcracker*, Paris in *Helen of Troy*, and in the *Blue Bird* and *Black Swan pas de deux*.

André Eglevsky has partnered most of the great ballerinas of the last twenty years: Danilova, Markova, Baronova, and Toumanova. As New York City Ballet's astonishing classical virtuoso, he became the partner of a new generation of ballerinas—Nora Kaye, Maria Tallchief, and Tanaquil LeClercq.

In *Sylvia: pas de deux*

Elaine Fifield

W HEN the Sadler's Wells Theatre Ballet toured America and Canada in 1951, critics were effusive over its vivacious young *prima ballerina*, Elaine Fifield. One of them called her "Margaret O'Brien with Danilova's legs"—an appelation that invariably gives this fun-loving girl the giggles. They praised her remarkable dancing, too, as have English critics ever since she made her first professional appearance in 1947.

Born in Sydney, Australia, in 1931, Elaine started in ballet school when she was eleven. On the day before her lessons began, she was taken to see her first real ballet, *Petrouchka*, which gave her an immediate objective to work toward—some day she, too, would dance on stage. Moreover, "the opportunity to express myself to music greatly appealed to me. I had studied the piano from a very early age, and have always had a great love for, and keen interest in, music."

She had studied only four years when she won the Overseas Scholarship of the Royal Academy of Dancing, which took her to England as a student at the Sadler's Wells School. Since her parents could not leave Australia, Elaine, a frightened, excited fifteen-year-old, set out alone to travel halfway around the world to London. At the School, Elaine proved herself a dancer of such unusual promise that just three weeks after her arrival she was taken into the newly formed Sadler's Wells Theatre Ballet as a student member.

She began to dance solos at once, her first being a small role in *The Gods Go A-Begging*. Elaine, to whom the whole theater routine was brand new, arrived backstage on the night of the performance just five minutes before curtain time. She was met by an excited and furious stage manager. Didn't she know, he stormed, that the first rule of the theater was that all dancers must be there

ELAINE FIFIELD. Above, in *Coppélia*

by "half hour call"? Sick and terrified at her blunder, Elaine scurried into her black mask and costume—and has never missed the "half hour call" since!

She won her first important solo that same year, in the summer of 1947 as Polka in *Façade*. "I adored dancing it," she says enthusiastically, "because I found the music so funny!"

Her first leading role, in *Les Sylphides*, a scant few months later, made the critics sit up and take notice. They watched her progress in a few short years to the position of *prima ballerina* with Sadler's Wells Theatre Ballet. Elaine was barely twenty!

British critics are unanimous in their praise of her. "She has a magnificently clean technique, and gives promise of becoming a truly great dancer," one of them wrote recently. Although she dances the classical ballets with great style and distinction, the roles in which she has been most enthusiastically acclaimed are those in which she displays her fine wit and piquant charm, such as the title role in *Pineapple Poll*.

Brown-eyed, black-haired Elaine is intelligent and serious about her career, saying that her favorite roles are "the most difficult ones, because I am not easily satisfied with my dancing." She is earnest and emphatic about what she calls "*un*helpful, *un*constructive criticism." Critics have a real duty toward dancers, she feels, and the dancer depends on the well-informed critic to point out her strength and her weaknesses. "How grateful I am to receive knowledgeable criticism!"

Young Fifield's hobbies are collecting operatic records, reading (especially Balzac), playing the piano, and eating chocolates! She likes to spend her vacations swimming and lazing in the sun with her husband, John Lanchbery, the company's conductor, whom she married in Los Angeles in 1951.

The two chief ambitions of this lively, lovely young ballerina are to have her parents (who are still in Australia) see her dance, and to "improve my dancing without losing my happiness."

Margot Fonteyn

THE ticket line stretched from the box office all around the block on the day tickets went on sale for the first American appearance of the Sadler's Wells Ballet in 1949. The entire series of performances in New York was completely sold out in advance, so eager were American ballet-lovers to see this famed English ballet company and the young star, Margot Fonteyn, upon whose sleek, dark head critics had often placed the supreme title of *prima ballerina assoluta.*

On the gala opening night at the Metropolitan Opera House, the audience settled into an expectant silence the instant Margot Fonteyn appeared on stage. The enchantment of the girl herself and the poetry of her dancing began to spread their magic to the farthest corners of the theater. The end of her first solo was greeted by a deafening storm of applause. Margot Fonteyn was all and more than New Yorkers had anticipated.

The whole Sadler's Wells company was superb, everyone agreed. Their four triumphant weeks at the Metropolitan led to their return engagement the following year for a cross-country tour. In each of the twenty-eight cities in which they appeared the story was the same—long lines at the box office, performances sold out in advance, and wildly enthusiastic audiences.

Hostesses vied with one another for the privilege of entertaining the stars at after-theater parties. Margot Fonteyn, looking every bit as glamorous as she looked on stage, was invariably the magnet of all eyes. Dramatically gowned, usually by Christian Dior, she was strikingly regal in appearance, but everyone who met her was disarmed by her friendly, modest manner. "How can she be so famous, and so unspoiled?" they asked each other in pleased surprise.

The few Americans who saw the great ballerina on more informal occasions saw the Margot that her fellow dancers and friends know and love—the unpredictable, high-spirited girl with a delightful sense of humor. Attired in practical tweeds and flat shoes, she did the sights with a vengeance, eagerly asking questions about everything. Exactly how high is the Empire State Building? How long is the Golden Gate Bridge? Is the Pump Room a good place to go dancing? She was a marvelous companion and a good sport, they found.

They discovered something else about her too—that she dismisses most of the superlative praise of her and her dancing as greatly exaggerated. She laughs at being called beautiful. "There is something wrong with all my features," she says matter-of-factly. Acutely self-critical of her dancing, she will rarely admit to being satisfied with her own performance: "No sooner do I correct one fault than another takes its place, if not two others!" Critics, who can find no fault with her, class her with the world's greatest dancers, Markova and Danilova, but Margot herself is unconvinced because her own impossible standards of perfection are not satisfied.

She was born Margaret Hookham in Reigate, England, in 1919. Her mother is of Brazilian-Irish extraction, and it is from her maiden name of Fontes that Margot later took the name of Fonteyn. Margot as a child traveled over much of the world because her father's work as a mining engineer took him to many far-off places. The Hookham family spent several years in Shanghai, and it was there, when Margot was five, that her mother took her to ballet school. Looking back, Margot "thinks" she enjoyed these lessons, but she had no particular desire to be a dancer—not even after her mother had taken her to see the world-famous Pavlova. But she worked at her lessons because she was a conscientious child.

Her family returned to England to settle down when Margot was thirteen. Her mother soon decided that it was time for her quiet, rather plump little daughter to begin making a serious career of ballet. Margot was enrolled in the Sadler's Wells School in 1932,

MARGOT FONTEYN in *Swan Lake*

where her first teachers remember her as a reserved, diffident child who showed no particular promise or even any great enthusiasm for dancing.

Her progress at the School for the next three years was slow and sure—and entirely unspectacular. But Ninette de Valois, the director of the School and its associated ballet company, began to notice this quiet adolescent, in whom she sensed something out of the ordinary. One day, watching Margot intent at the practice *barre*, de Valois made a prophetic announcement. "That child," she said, "has talent." No one else at the School could yet see it, and certainly Margot herself had no feeling of destiny.

Her first appearance on the Sadler's Wells stage went completely unnoticed, for Margot was one of the thirty-two little snow-flakes in *The Nutcracker*. Her first solo role—Creole Girl in *Rio Grande*—was a creditable job, but far from a sensation. But after her lovely, classical Mazurka in *Les Sylphides*, members of the company began to say among themselves that perhaps De Valois was right.

Young Margot herself was confused and frightened at all these performances, feeling far from ready for the solos that began to come her way. There was only one really great dancer in the world, Margot earnestly believed, and that was Alicia Markova, the *prima ballerina* of Sadler's Wells. She studied Markova's every move during class, rehearsal, and performance. Markova was her idol and her ideal. To think that she herself could ever approximate such beauty was beyond the bounds of her imagination.

When Markova left Sadler's Wells in 1935, Margot, along with four or five other rising young dancers, was given some of her leading roles. When she was seventeen, she danced the role of Giselle, in which the lyric beauty of her dancing and the sureness and sensitivity of her interpretation were an astonishing revelation to everyone. De Valois, after watching her that night, knew then that her prophecy would be fulfilled—Margot Fonteyn, the company's first home-trained ballerina, was destined to shine as brilliantly as her predecessor, Markova.

Season by season, as she added role after role to her repertoire, British ballet-goers became increasingly aware that Fonteyn was developing into a dancer of astonishing caliber. Frederick Ashton, England's leading choreographer, began to create ballets for her even before she was sixteen. In his first, the English version of *Le Baiser de la Fée,* Margot scored a tremendous and moving success as The Ice Maiden. In the years that have followed, Ashton has created more than fifteen ballets for her, among them such immediate favorites as: *Apparitions, Dante Sonata, The Wise Virgins, The Wanderer,* and *Cinderella.*

As the fame of Britain's own ballerina began to spread, she was asked to appear as guest artist at La Scala in Milan, at Les Ballets de Paris, and at the Royal Danish Ballet. The royal family of England came often to see her dance. Her audiences adored her with that mixture of affectionate indulgence and enormous pride which the English show for their favorites. When a foot injury kept her from dancing for some time, her return was greeted wildly, and the concern about her foot was widespread and personal.

Margot Fonteyn was now a celebrity, whether she liked it or not, and the company's triumphant visits to the United States in 1949 and 1950 added to the glamour that was inescapably linked to her name. Sadler's Wells's gala homecoming performance at Covent Garden was attended by Queen Elizabeth, then princess, who invited Fonteyn to the Royal Box to congratulate her warmly on her American success.

To the quiet, unmannered perfection of Margot Fonteyn's technique was added a new, warmer maturity that enriched every role she danced. Arnold Haskell, Britain's top critic, says: "Fonteyn has the greatest range in contemporary ballet, from the sparkle of *Swan Lake* and the pure romance of *Les Sylphides* to the modern sophistication of *A Wedding Bouquet.* In *Giselle,* she gives the most memorable performance to be seen in ballet today."

Almost heedless of the heights she has reached, Margot continues to lead a disciplined life of work and routine. Her day begins early each morning when she leaves her pleasant London apartment (filled with fine antiques, bric-a-brac, and her collection of china cats) for her first class or rehearsal. Although no two days are the same, each is completely taken up with preparations for the night's performance.

Each night, she arrives at the theater at least two and a half hours before curtain time. First she puts on make-up, with special emphasis on the slanting outlines of her brilliant dark eyes. Then she warms up at the practice *barre*. She is grave and intent as she stands in the wings waiting for her cue, for she still suffers from acute pre-curtain nervousness. After she has taken her last curtain call, she is swept by a flood of relief that it is all over.

Her many friends, her public, and the critics worry about her. Is she working too hard? Is she taking proper care of her chronic foot-ailment? Are the choreographers doing her justice in the ballets they create for her? One London critic wrote recently, like an anxious, doting uncle: "She takes risks on the stage which, as feats of daring, let alone beauty, are alarming. Margot cannot last forever at this pitch."

A dancer's career is a short one, Margot herself says quite practically, and she has to work while she can. Later, there will be time to relax. In the meantime, she wants to "continue what I am doing until age or misadventure stops me." There are already scattered rumors that she may retire before long, but for every prophet who insists that she will quit at the peak of her career, there are two who say that Margot Fonteyn could no more stop dancing than she could stop breathing.

"For her movements are as natural as those of any creature in his own element: the flight of the bird through cool space, the fish gliding through crystal water, the wild cat slipping like a shadow through tangled jungle. There seems no reason why anything should cause a break in this continuity of movement—soft as an endless cascade of silk, sweet and smooth as the uncoiling of honey poured slowly from a bottomless jar." *

* Reprinted, by permission of William Chappell, from his book: *Fonteyn—Impressions of a Ballerina*.

Frederic Franklin

LIVELY, witty Frederic Franklin has been called the most likable chap in ballet. He has also been called the most versatile. "Freddie can dance *anything*," his friends say with matter-of-fact pride, and the success of his richly varied career bears them out.

Franklin, who was born in Liverpool, England, in 1914, danced for the first time in public when he was six, before he had a single lesson. He was so pleased with his first taste of publicity that he started taking ballet lessons at once with "a Mrs. Kelly"—lessons which he says he loved so much that he could think of nothing else. Blond, blue-eyed little Freddie, with his engaging grin and bubbling personality, soon became a familiar sight in and around Liverpool, dancing in clubs, cabarets, and pageants.

When he was seventeen, a tall, poised young man of considerable accomplishments, Freddie blithely set out for London. He was already a skillful dancer, proficient pianist, and passable actor, and had directed his own classes in ballroom dancing. But Freddie was looking for new worlds to conquer. He joined a troupe called The Lancashire Lads, and almost at once found himself in Paris. The Lads were booked in a revue at the Casino de Paris, where Freddie also danced with Mistinguette, the fabulous singing-dancing star, and occasionally accompanied her on the piano.

Back in London, he kept right on going—dancing first in a series of musical comedies and then in London's most exclusive night club with the lovely English dancer, Wendy Toye. But the desire had been growing in the back of his mind to be a real ballet dancer. To prepare himself, he went to one of the finest Russian ballet teachers, Nicholas Legat, and later to Mme Pruzina, former teacher of Pavlova.

The break he had been hoping for came as a result of his expert dancing in the play, *Ballerina,* in which Anton Dolin was the star. Dolin, already making plans to found a ballet company with Alicia Markova, told Franklin there would be a place for him in the new company. The Markova-Dolin Company opened in 1935, and Freddie was a soloist. After little more than a year, he became the official understudy for Dolin himself.

The closing night of the last season of the Markova-Dolin Company in 1937 proved to be a beginning for Franklin, instead of an ending. In the audience that night, intently watching the brilliant young man who danced the Trepak in *The Nutcracker,* was Leonide Massine, ballet master and choreographer of the Ballet Russe de Monte Carlo. He went backstage after the performance and offered Franklin a position as one of the principal dancers with the Ballet Russe de Monte Carlo!

Young Franklin was dizzy with his good fortune, for to him the Ballet Russe was "the best company in the whole world," and he would be dancing with the greatest dancers of the day: Danilova, Toumanova, Youskevitch, and Lifar. He made his debut with the company in Monte Carlo in 1938, dancing a dashing role —the Baron in Massine's new ballet *Gaité Parisienne,* in which his charm and assurance made him an instant favorite. His American debut, in the identical role later in the same year, won him an enthusiastic host of new admirers. From then on, this versatile dancer was immensely popular with both American and Continental audiences, dancing in such widely assorted ballets as *Prince Igor, Le Beau Danube,* and *Rouge et Noir.*

The company was in England rehearsing a new Ashton ballet, *Devil's Holiday,* scheduled for its *première* in New York within a few short weeks, when World War II broke out. In the resultant confusion, the dancers took whatever passage they could get, and sailed from England in small groups. Franklin, one of the last to leave, arrived in New York at noon on the actual day of the Metropolitan Opera House opening. Still groggy from the after-effects of seasickness, and with no time for full rehearsal, he danced his difficult lead role, the Beggar, in *Devil's Holiday.* The ballet and Franklin were a great success.

FREDERIC FRANKLIN in *Le Beau Danube*

His diverse talents, increasingly evident as the years went on, made him the top dancer in the Ballet Russe de Monte Carlo, and his unfailing good nature made him a general favorite with all the dancers. No matter how pressing his own schedule, he always had time to help young dancers with new roles or to give a word of encouragement to a discouraged youngster. It was a logical move, and a most popular one, when thirty-year-old Franklin was made ballet master of the company in 1944—the only non-Russian ever to hold such a position with a "Russian" company.

Franklin left the Ballet Russe de Monte Carlo in 1952, after fourteen years. With red-haired Mia Slavenska he formed the Slavenska-Franklin Ballet, which opened in Philadelphia in the fall of 1952.

Biggest hit of the new company's repertoire was a colorful, melodramatic ballet version of *A Streetcar Named Desire,* where Freddie Franklin displayed the same youthful vigor and dash that have always characterized him. Audiences were electrified, and critics remarked that "veterans Slavenska and Franklin gave the performances of their lives!"

Beryl Grey

But . . . hush . . . the spirit comes . . .
     the gates unclose.
What is she thinking of, this floating flower?
Is she but keeping every nerve intent
On movement strained to graces, and the air?
Is she withinly happy in her power,
A thousand watchers making her aware
That they are hers, to govern by a hair,
Hers to a heart, as to an angel sent? *

WHEN John Masefield wrote this tribute to one of England's top ballerinas, he put into words what all British ballet-goers feel about lovely young Beryl Grey. They are indeed "hers to a heart"—their first, very own baby ballerina.

Fame's spotlight focused on Beryl Grey when she was still a child of fourteen. The scene was Oxford, England, where the Sadler's Wells Ballet was on tour. Margot Fonteyn was to dance the leads in *Les Sylphides, Façade,* and *The Gods Go A-Begging,* but a last-minute injury incapacitated her. Fledgling Beryl Grey was hastily substituted in all three roles. Astonished to learn that she was to be the star that evening, Beryl's first instinctive re-action was a wave of fright, which rapidly gave way to pure joy at the thought of dancing. This joy, which dancing always brings her, carried the fourteen-year-old buoyantly through what could have been a difficult ordeal. The audience took her to its heart at once.

* Reprinted by permission of John Masefield, Poet Laureate of England, from his "Beryl Grey as Prelude in *Les Sylphides.*"

Ballet has been the reason for her life from the time she can first remember. Born Beryl Groom in Highgate, London, in 1927, she started to ballet school when she was four years old because several of her friends were going. Attractive little Beryl, with her shining black hair and sweet, heart-shaped face, was the much-admired star of her class from the first.

Then one day her mother took her to see a real ballet in London—*Les Sylphides*. From the top gallery, this child with the dreaming eyes drank in the fairyland spread out before her and longed with all her heart to be a part of it.

When she was nine, she enrolled at the Sadler's Wells Ballet School in Islington. She worked devotedly for the next few years, and felt with happy certainty that she would soon be ready for her first appearance in the *corps de ballet*. But war abruptly changed all that. In 1940, the Sadler's Wells Theatre was taken over as a rest center for bombed-out Islington families, and the school was closed.

Young Beryl was crushed. Forlornly, she tried to adjust herself to the idea that now she could never be a ballerina. What would she do with her life? Half-heartedly, this serious child of thirteen decided that the next best thing would be to become a doctor. But a few months later she heard the joyful news that the school was to reopen in a new location. Beryl was waiting at the door the day the school opened.

Soon she was ready for her first real performance—in the *corps de ballet* in *Giselle*. Only a year later, when she was fourteen, she had her unexpected chance to substitute for Fonteyn.

Beryl's own first ballerina role was a dream come true, for she starred in the same ballet that had enchanted her as a child—*Les Sylphides*. Two months later, on her fifteenth birthday, she danced the demanding dual role of Odette-Odile in the full-length version of *Swan Lake*. Her wicked Odile blazed with unexpected fire, in startling contrast to the gentle sweetness of her Odette, and her whole performance drew an ovation from the New Theatre audience.

BERYL GREY in *Giselle*

She began to dance leading roles in the company's new ballets: *The Quest, Promenade.* She won considerable notice in 1944 when she danced the title role in *Giselle,* and again, just after her nineteenth birthday, when she appeared as Princess Aurora in the full-length version of *Sleeping Beauty.*

The critics, who all along had treated her with affection and watchful pride, began to go overboard. They praised the ease and fluency of her dancing, and remarked upon her "sincerity and humility, which are the two prime attributes of any great artist." One critic said: "I see no other dancer capable of giving so much untrammeled, uninhibited outpouring of joyous dancing for the sake of dancing."

Beryl Grey is very tall for a ballerina (5-feet-6), a height that might be a handicap for another dancer, but in her case, critics point out, it only enhances the beauty of her *line.* Their only worry is that partners of sufficient height and strength may not always be found to dance with her.

A glamorous being to those who watch her dance, Beryl Grey leads a very simple life offstage. She rarely goes out after a performance, preferring to eat a quiet supper at home with her young husband, a Swedish doctor whom she married in 1950. Occasionally, they go to concerts, plays, or art galleries. But the best evenings of all are those "with just the two of us in our own flat." On those evenings, Beryl likes to cook the special dishes her husband enjoys, play the piano, at which she is quite accomplished, or listen to their collection of classical records.

Beryl Grey has an ordered plan for the future. She wants to dance as guest artist with other companies "in as many countries as possible." She wants to star in a "first-class film" because she liked her first taste of movie-making in 1952: *The Black Swan,* the first three-dimensional ballet film. She wants to continue her many public appearances on television, radio, and even the lecture stand.

It is a busy life she foresees. But one feels that whatever her dreams and ambitions, nothing is beyond the reach of this enchanting girl who looks so serenely at the world before her.

Robert Helpmann

THE distinguished career of Robert Helpmann, *premier danseur,* has been almost matched by that of Robert Helpmann, actor. As an actor Helpmann has starred in movies and on the legitimate stage, and as a dancer he has been England's top favorite for close to twenty years.

Robert Murray Helpmann was born in Mount Gambier, Australia, in 1909, and his love of the theater began, literally, when he was still an infant. His mother, who was an amateur actress of considerable talent, used to read Shakespeare to him long before he knew what the words meant. The beautiful flow of the poetry and the high-sounding phrases delighted him, and Robert, who was an intensely impressionable child, learned to love acting and the theater with all his heart.

Little Bobby hated the dull restrictions of school, and lived only for Saturday of each week, when he could go to the matinee at the local theater. It did not matter in the least what was showing as long as he could be there.

He began to study dancing after he entered Prince Alfred's College in Adelaide, taking lessons every Saturday in what was called "fancy dancing." He made his first public appearance when he was fourteen, as a solo dancer in a small musical comedy, and today recalls this performance as "very energetic and madly passionate!" He marked time impatiently for the next three years, looking for somewhere to dance or act, or both, and finally joined an Australian touring company as a "dancing actor." He spent five years touring the Australian continent with this company, tremendously satisfied with being a professional.

But when he saw the great Anna Pavlova dance in a recital in Sydney, he found out, with a shock, how much he had to learn as a dancer. Wangling a job in the *corps de ballet* of her company, he

toured for eighteen months, never missing a rehearsal or performance, even when he was not appearing himself. The polished perfection of Pavlova and her partner filled him with a driving need to
learn everything he could about ballet.

When he was twenty-three Bobby set out for London, determined to get into the Sadler's Wells School. Dame Ninette de Valois, its director, vividly remembers the day in 1932 when the slim,
rather small young man with the remarkably expressive face presented himself to her at the studio. She accepted this "polite and
quite self-assured" young man as a pupil, and Robert Helpmann
began the vigorous ballet training that he had come across the
world to find.

Bobby, his teachers soon found, had a remarkably quick in-
telligence and an unflagging eagerness to learn. They found, too,
that the young man had an amazingly supple body, a feeling for
music which made his movements flow, and a strong grace in spite
of his lack of great physical strength. But most of all, they saw and
developed Robert Helpmann's instinct for drama.

In 1933, just six months after he had arrived in London,
Bobby Helpmann was taken from the school into the *corps de ballet* of the Vic-Wells company. His first leading role (Satan) was in
De Valois's ballet *Job*. Next came the role of Hilarion in *Giselle*.
De Valois, pleased with her rapidly developing actor-dancer, built
a leading role especially for him in her *Haunted Ballroom* in 1934,
in which he gained his first substantial critical acclaim. In Helpmann, the critics announced, an English dancer of considerable
dramatic scope had been discovered.

He was regularly teamed with the company's star, Alicia
Markova, until she left in 1935, and after that partnered the rising
new star, Margot Fonteyn. They were a popular pair from the first
time they appeared together, and British ballet-goers often shouted
from the gallery for their favorites, "Bobby" and "Margot."

Much as Helpmann was admired for his pure classical technique, both he and his audiences reveled in the roles where he
could show off his humor and his passion for characterization. Au-

ROBERT HELPMANN and MARGOT FONTEYN in *Giselle*

diences delighted in his elaborate make-ups (all of which he does himself) and in his motley assortment of costumes and wigs. They loved Helpmann as the ravaged, tortured Rake in *The Rake's Progress;* as the doddering, bewildered toy-maker Coppelius in *Coppélia;* as the dandified gentleman in *A Wedding Bouquet;* and especially as the clowning Mr. O'Reilly in *The Prospect Before Us.*

Helpmann's innate love of the dramatic propelled him naturally into choreography. His first work was *Comus,* in 1942, in which he danced the title role, and several months later he did the choreography for a ballet version of a play that had long interested him: *Hamlet.* Helpmann himself danced the Melancholy Dane and Margot Fonteyn was Ophelia.

His next choreography, *Miracle in the Gorbals* (concerned with the return of Christ to the world of today), is the most outstanding of his ballets. Helpmann, a perfectionist, spent hours in the London slums, making mental notes of the public-house types that were later reproduced with startling effect in his ballet. The result was a work about which a controversy has raged ever since, but British critic Arnold Haskell says it "must rank as one of the outstanding creations of contemporary ballet."

Helpmann's helpless infatuation with Shakespeare led him into the straight acting version of *Hamlet* at the Old Vic Theatre in 1944. Here, again, critics were divided. They agreed that he had a speaking voice of grave beauty, that his timing was perfect and all of his movements were poetry—but his acting as Hamlet caused no great stir.

Thoroughly bitten with the acting bug, Helpmann made several movies: *Henry V* with Laurence Olivier, *The Red Shoes* and *Tales of Hoffmann* with Moira Shearer, and one with the English comedian Alec Guinness. American audiences, who knew him from these movies, welcomed him eagerly when Sadler's Wells Ballet toured the United States in 1949 and 1950. His inspired foolery as one of the ugly sisters in the ballet *Cinderella* was a particular American favorite, as were his performances in *Caesar and Cleopatra* and *Antony and Cleopatra.* Audiences applauded his magnificent Prince in *The Sleeping Beauty* and in *Swan Lake*, and each *pas de deux* that he and Margot Fonteyn danced brought down the house.

Within Sadler's Wells Ballet, which is his professional home, Robert Helpmann is devotedly admired as a dancer and heartily liked as a person. His ready wit, quick, amusing speech, and warm liking for people have won him friends everywhere. He is immensely energetic, and keeps up on everything that is going on in the theater. He is fascinated by the various techniques of actors, especially his favorite comedians, Alec Guinness and Danny Kaye. His own amazingly detailed characterizations are enriched by his study of other actors and by his continuous reading, especially of Dickens and of modern psychological studies.

British ballet critic Audrey Williamson has said of him: "His brain, his theatrical instinct, his sense of fun and eye for character have combined to form him as an actor who does not need the aid of speech to make his part live." Robert Helpmann is, without question, England's most outstanding actor-dancer.

Rosella Hightower

"THE most enchanting of Enchanted Princesses," the critics called Rosella Hightower after her first performance in *Princess Aurora*. Everyone who has ever seen her dance has found her not only enchanting, but beautiful. Yet Rosella herself insists that when she was growing up she was beset with fears that she was "too ugly" ever to dance the great romantic roles!

The daughter of a Cherokee Indian father and a Scotch-Irish mother, she was born in 1920 in Ardmore, Oklahoma. As a child she ran free and wild on her parents' farm, but when she reached school age the family moved to Kansas City, Missouri. Rosella, freckle-faced and spindle-legged, was a real tomboy, and her mother enrolled her at the Perkins School of the Dance when she was nine in a hopeful attempt to make a little lady of her.

Rosella fretted at being made to dress up and go to ballet class. But once there she took an instant liking to her teacher, Dorothy Perkins. It was Miss Perkins who first saw in this half-Indian, half-elfin child the latent qualities that were to make her a great ballerina. In speaking of her beloved "Perky," Rosella says now: "She was not only a dancing teacher, she was a general education."

At last, when the girl was eighteen, Perky told her she was ready to become a professional dancer. Arrangements were made, plans completed, and Rosella was on board ship heading for France and the Ballet Russe de Monte Carlo.

Naïve, unsophisticated Rosella, suddenly transported to glittering Monte Carlo, found the abrupt change from her humdrum Middle-Western existence almost too exciting to bear. The first day, when she stood at the practice *barre* in the great casino, she was dizzy with unbelief as she looked around her. Could this be plain Rosella Hightower from Oklahoma, in the same room with

ROSELLA HIGHTOWER in *Scherzo*

the greatest dancers in the world? These glamorous figures had long been her idols—Markova, Massine, Danilova, Franklin, Youskevitch—and here they all were! "I was the last dancer in the line of the *corps de ballet*," she recalls, a smile lighting her gray-green eyes, "but for me it was complete, unadulterated bliss."

Rosella was in a whirl of delight that whole first year, touring the great cities of Europe and America. The climax of the year for her was the company's arrival in Kansas City. Rosella was home— as a real ballet dancer, and ballet master Massine gave the girl her first solo role in honor of the occasion. The evening of the performance was one excitement after another—her dancing as Papillon in

Carnaval, her joyful reunion backstage with Perky, and, to top it all off, Massine's high praise and his announcement that the role was to be hers from then on.

Rosella continued touring the United States with the Ballet Russe de Monte Carlo for two years, and in each city the critics took increasing notice of this young soloist. Her dancing came to the attention of Lucia Chase, co-director of Ballet Theatre, who invited Rosella to join her company in 1942. Just one year later, she danced her first ballerina role—Odette in *Swan Lake*.

Critics everywhere began to prophesy a brilliant future for her. Rosella added role after role to her repertoire in the four years she was with Ballet Theatre: Swanhilda in *Coppélia*, Blue Bird in *Princess Aurora*, Calliope in *Apollo*, Boulotte in *Bluebeard*, Impromptu Dance in *Graduation Ball*. Now the critics cried: "An astonishing virtuoso!"

Then, in quick succession, she danced with three different companies in as many seasons: Massine's Ballet Russe Highlights, the Markova-Dolin Company, and the Original Ballet Russe. In the early summer of 1947, the Marquis George de Cuevas picked Rosella as one of the ballerinas for his newly organized company, the De Cuevas Grand Ballet.

Rosella is today the top-ranking ballerina with this company, and the wife of handsome Jean Robier, portrait painter and costume designer, to whom she was married in 1950. They live in a studio apartment in Paris.

With her young husband, fun-loving Rosella is enjoying again the energetic outdoor life that she loved in her tomboy youth—horseback riding, skiing in the Alps, and swimming. When the company is touring, Rosella and Jean travel in their own car—a sleek Jaguar that is their most prized possession.

Rosella Hightower, dancing in such new ballets as *Tarasiana*, *Doña Inez de Castro*, and *Coup de Feu*, displays a technique that is flawless, an interpretation that is brilliant, and a personal magnetism that illumines her every move. Rosella Hightower wears with grace her title of one of the world's greatest ballerinas.

Renée Jeanmaire

"**B**ROADWAY BOWLED OVER BY BALLET!" So ran the headlines in *Variety*, the Bible of show business, one day late in 1949. Two imported ballet troupes, the article reported, were currently the biggest box-office hits in New York. One was Sadler's Wells Ballet, the other Les Ballets de Paris, whose chief attraction was the impudent young French ballerina, Renée Jeanmaire.

Audiences packed New York's Winter Garden for four months to see her in Les Ballets de Paris's version of *Carmen*, in which she romped with splendid abandon, partnered by Roland Petit. In this, her first appearance in the United States, young Jeanmaire created much the same kind of delighted stir which had followed her in Europe.

Born in Paris in 1924, Renée Jeanmaire began her ballet training at the ballet school of the Paris Opéra when she was eleven, as a *petit rat*. She advanced into the Opéra Ballet company itself when she was fifteen, and worked there under ballet master Serge Lifar.

After eight years with the Opéra Ballet, Jeanmaire joined Col. de Basil's Ballet Russe de Monte Carlo as soloist. Then, in the summer of 1944, she danced briefly with the Nouveau Ballet de Monte Carlo and was acclaimed for her performances in *Coppélia*, *La Fille Mal Gardée*, and as The Top in *Aubade*.

Late in 1944 Jeanmaire appeared with Roland Petit in a series of his experimental ballets. These performances—much talked-about in postwar Paris—led to the founding of Petit's own company, Les Ballets des Champs-Élysées, in which Jeanmaire alternated leading roles with several other exceptional young ballerinas.

When Roland Petit sent this small company off on tour, Jeanmaire remained behind to join him in a second new company, Les Ballets de Paris. They went to work on Petit's version of *Carmen*, in which Jeanmaire was to dance the title role.

Petit's *Carmen* was an unconventional ballet that ignored the opera and libretto, being composed of scenes imagined by the choreographer. Jeanmaire was a little concerned about the daring love scenes in which she was to star, and by the time she arrived in London for the *première*, she was in a state of nervous apprehension as to how the ballet would be received. But at the end of the performance on opening night, the conservative London audience was in a delighted uproar, calling Jeanmaire and Petit back for eighteen curtain calls. *Carmen* played for six months before going on to Paris and New York.

From New York, Jeanmaire and Petit went on to Hollywood. The film *Hans Christian Andersen* was in the making, and when Moira Shearer dropped out of the cast because she was expecting a baby, her role was given to Jeanmaire. When she reported at the movie studio, "Zizi" Jeanmaire, who had been dubbed by the press "a firecracker in dancing tights," turned out to be a surprise. Instead of the temperamental *artiste* that her press notices had led everyone to expect, she was a quiet, friendly young woman, who arrived accompanied by her mother. Directly after the formalities of studio introductions were over, she asked in her charmingly accented voice: "And now, please, where is it the practice room?" This serious intentness on the business at hand continued to delight and impress her co-workers during the filming of the movie.

By the time the shooting of *Hans Christian Andersen* was finished, Jeanmaire was homesick for France. She flew home as soon as the studio released her, returning only briefly to New York for the movie's glittering *première*. With the release of *Hans Christian Andersen,* in which Jeanmaire gave an appealing performance opposite Danny Kaye and danced with Roland Petit, many American movie-goers were treated to their first glimpse of this provocative young French ballerina.

In 1954, Jeanmaire was back on Broadway, making dance history as the star of the musical *The Girl in Pink Tights*. A new movie, another musical, and a TV show of her own are in the works for "Zizi" Jeanmaire, whose captivating performances have placed her in the front rank of dramatic ballerinas.

RENÉE JEANMAIRE and ROLAND PETIT in *The Little Mermaid* ballet from the
motion picture *Hans Christian Andersen*

Nora Kaye

THERE was a near-riot at the staid Metropolitan Opera House on the historic night of April 8, 1942, the like of which has rarely been seen in American ballet. From the last row of the gallery to the orchestra pit rose a bedlam of shouting, stamping, and applause that showed no signs of ever letting up.

Backstage, too, excitement and confusion ran high. Dancers hugged each other with joy and the wings buzzed with excited chatter. The center of the clamor was a slim, brown-haired dancer in an old-fashioned yellow dress, who accepted her comrades' congratulations with an almost tremulous smile–of happiness. Each time the applause swelled to a new climax, friendly hands pushed her out on stage for another curtain call—there were twenty-six in all. And still the ovation roared on—quieted only by the management's firm refusal to raise the curtain again.

The cause of this riot was the *première* of Antony Tudor's modern masterpiece, *Pillar of Fire*, in which Ballet Theatre's Nora Kaye had danced the dramatic role of Hagar. The story of *Pillar of Fire* is built around Hagar, a sensitive and repressed young girl who is the pawn of her two sisters: a bitter old maid and a malicious coquette. The Youngest Sister deliberately lures Hagar's sweetheart (the Friend) away from her, and Hagar, in despair, lets herself be seduced by the local lady-killer (the Young Man from the House Opposite). Then, overwhelmed by wild and unendurable guilt, she runs from the Friend in shame. But he catches and holds her with understanding gentleness, and Hagar's troubled soul finds peace at last in his love. In bare outline, this story is simplicity itself, but the complexity of the characters and their emotions, expressed by pantomime alone, make *Pillar of Fire* "a tremendous work which nobody, not even Tudor himself, has yet succeeded in topping." *

* Arnold Haskell

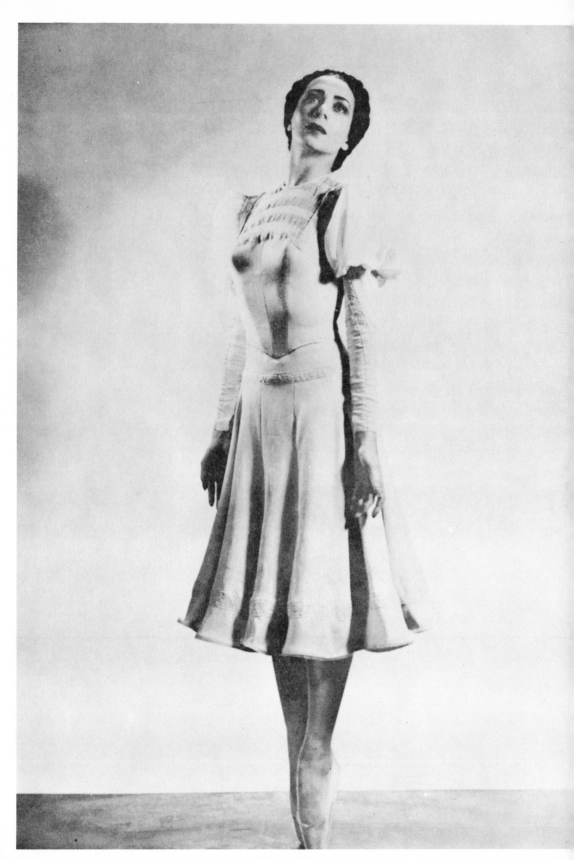

NORA KAYE as Hagar

The entire cast that night was near-perfect: Hugh Laing as the Young Man, Antony Tudor as the Friend, Lucia Chase as the Eldest Sister, and Annabelle Lyon as the Youngest Sister. But *Pillar of Fire* was unmistakably Hagar's drama, and Nora Kaye danced it with a tragic intensity that moved everyone who saw her.

With that one performance, Nora Kaye stood revealed as a dramatic dancer without peer. She danced in *Pillar of Fire* for eight years with Ballet Theatre, and her Hagar became a living legend. When she danced it in England, critics called it "the greatest individual performance to be seen in England." In recent years there have been satisfactory substitutions in some of the other parts, but it is impossible to conceive of Hagar without Kaye.

Lovers of American ballet are proud of the fact that this great dramatic ballerina is entirely an American product. Nora Kaye was born in New York, trained in American ballet schools, and has always danced with American companies. Her parents were Russian, and when Nora first began to dance she used the name of her actor-father—Koreff. She later amended it to Koreff-Kay, and finally to simply Kaye.

She began studying ballet for the age-old reason: "Mother wanted me to." When she was eight, she enrolled for daily classes at the Metropolitan Opera Ballet School. Nora Kaye says today that she always worked hard at these early lessons, "because I wanted to be first in my class." She began to appear in many children's roles in opera ballets. "I was an elf, a peasant child, a gnome —oh, all kinds of things," she says vaguely.

These tiny parts gradually became larger parts, so that the transition to the solo roles that followed was natural and easy. Even then her ability was so marked that, with her teachers' encouragement, she soon added three lessons a week with the great Russian choreographer and teacher Michel Fokine. It was her association with this tremendously stimulating teacher that cemented her decision, when she was fifteen, to be a dancer. She enrolled at the School of American Ballet, where she studied with George Balanchine and Pierre Vladimiroff. Then for a year she danced with the American Ballet Company at the Metropolitan.

When Ballet Theatre was founded in 1939, Nora Kaye joined as a member of the *corps de ballet*. Her first lead role came two years later in *Gala Performance*, where, as the temperamental Russian Ballerina, she showed a remarkable and delightful flair for comedy. Then, when she was just twenty-two, came her dramatic triumph in *Pillar of Fire*. Her next success, in *Dim Lustre*, showed a new Nora Kaye—a gay sophisticate who was a startling contrast to the brooding Hagar. In *Apollo* (1943), *On Stage!* (1945), and *Facsimile* (1946) she scored one success after another, and in the classic *Swan Lake* and *Giselle* showed a lovely romantic quality that was unexpected.

Kaye left Ballet Theatre in 1951 to join America's brightest and newest company, the New York City Ballet. Here she continued the Nora Kaye tradition of success in *Symphony in C*, *Bourrée Fantasque*, and *Mother Goose Suite*. As The Novice in *The Cage* she met a frenzied reception that came close to matching that of *Pillar of Fire*.

She has appeared in several musicals: *Virginia, Great Lady, Stars in Your Eyes*, and the Bette Davis show, *Two's Company*. She accepted these parts, she says, "because I enjoy doing all kinds of new things."

Nora Kaye herself is an informal, chic, and sophisticated young woman who lives in a fashionable midtown New York hotel with her tiny Yorkshire terrier, Mandy. Mandy, her doting mistress reports, was "the size of a mouse" when she was born, and now full grown is "not quite as big as a lamb roast!"

An extremely good-looking young woman, Kaye has the mobile face of an actress, reflecting her every mood. Her face is radiant when she speaks of ballet and the joy she feels in "expressing an emotion through body movement, without words." Her fascination with drama and pantomime, and her extraordinary ability to portray complex and moving characters, are the very foundation of Nora Kaye's art. Her place as America's foremost actress-ballerina is undisputed.

John Kriza

JOHN KRIZA dances, as he does everything else, because it is *fun*. He likes everything about his life as a *premier danseur*, even living constantly out of suitcases. Travel suits him fine, he says with his sudden, flashing grin, because there's a lot of the gypsy in him.

Kriza's carefree enjoyment is obvious the moment he leaps on stage with his dark hair flying. The audience, infected by his enthusiasm, enjoys itself right along with him. Here is a man, they feel instantly, who is doing just what he was meant to do!

He was born in 1919 in Berwyn, Illinois, of Czechoslovakian parents. John was a sickly child, and his mother hopefully enrolled him in ballet school to build up his strength. His father, who was a butcher, hooted with derision at the idea of his son dancing, but the lessons continued regardless. Right from the start, although John liked to dance, he dreaded the teasing and tormenting he had to take from his friends because of it. To ward off the dread taunts of "sissy," he developed a protective swagger and a slight belligerence that sometimes show through his easy charm even today. But now he has powerful shoulders and a stocky, muscular physique that would do credit to a football halfback.

After several years of more concentrated study with Bentley Stone in Chicago, he set out to conquer the world. But, with the country in the depths of the great depression, it was a bad time to look for a job. There were a dozen clamoring applicants for any job of any kind, and for a ballet dancer with no experience there were no jobs.

Young John Kriza kept right on looking. He found a few brief dancing jobs, without pay. Then one bright day he met Ruth Page, director of the Chicago WPA Dance Project and of the Chicago Civic Opera Ballet, who granted him an audition. As a result, John got his first paying job in the *corps de ballet* with the WPA Dance

JOHN KRIZA in *Facsimile*

Project. Before long, he was off for a tour of South America with the Chicago Civic Opera Ballet.

The tour ended all too soon from John's point of view. Back in New York again in 1939, he was broke and without a job. Via the grapevine, he learned that a new company, Ballet Theatre, was being organized. John auditioned immediately and was accepted. He danced with Ballet Theatre for a season, and then joined Ballet Caravan for a summer tour of South America.

Aboard the ship heading for home, after the tour was over, John was asking himself the same old question: "Where do we go from here?" That question was answered when a telegram was handed to him just as the ship approached New York's harbor: "Report to Ballet Theatre immediately." Kriza, the first one down the gangplank, rushed bag and baggage to the theater, where he learned that the company needed him for a performance that very night. After only the sketchiest of rehearsals, he danced in *Gala Performance* and *Beloved*. Since then, John has quit worrying about tomorrow. It always takes care of itself, says he!

In three years, John Kriza progressed from the *corps de ballet* to soloist. Then, on a memorable night in 1944 at the Metropolitan Opera House, he danced his first leading role—in the *première* of the rollicking *Fancy Free*. That ballet, the story of three happy-go-lucky sailors on shore leave, was a hit from the moment the sailors bounded on stage. Jerome Robbins, Harold Lang, and John Kriza, the Sailors, won deafening applause that night for their highly individual and marvelously high-spirited characterizations. At one point, the audience was so beside itself with enthusiasm that it applauded for five solid minutes while the ballet went on. The *première* was a triumph for all concerned, and especially for John Kriza, who made his mark that night as a dancer of enormous ability and charm. He remembers, almost with unbelief, that the great gold curtain of the Metropolitan went up and down twenty-six times for the curtain calls.

Since then, during the years he has been dancing in *Fancy Free* with Ballet Theatre, he has had some twenty different sets of sailor partners, but Kriza's performance remains as spontaneous and humorous as ever. His own special delight in the role has never lessened.

From that night on, he was a favorite with Ballet Theatre audiences, who were captivated by his flashing good looks and the verve and easy humor of his dancing. He created the leading roles in *Interplay* and *Facsimile*, and later danced the leads in *Pillar of Fire* and *Billy the Kid*. Critics, who admire him tremendously in these spirited roles, admire him almost equally in classical ballets. Kriza says he enjoys the challenge of an occasional classical role, but enjoys far more the feeling of "letting himself go" in the modern American ballets in which he first made a name for himself.

His summers are spent having fun in the Kriza manner. Between seasons, he hunts for any kind of dancing job, because, as he puts it: "I don't like not to be working." He spent one summer dancing in the musical *Panama Hattie*. He did a couple of nightclub engagements in Chicago and New York with Ruth Ann Koesun (who also dances with him in Ballet Theatre). He has done summer stock in Cohasset and vaudeville in Chicago. He spent the summer of 1952 dancing in the musical *Kiss Me, Kate*. He has appeared on many television shows, sometimes dancing, sometimes being interviewed. He says without hesitation that he prefers the dancing spots on television—because he gets paid for them!

Between these varied assignments, he flies off for a few days to his dairy farm in Wheaton, near Chicago. "It's lots of fun to switch from being a dancer to being a farmer," he maintains. And quite a switch it is, from grease paint and ballet slippers and footlights to blue jeans, work shoes, and hot sunshine. Kriza happily runs the tractor, milks his twenty cows, and revels in all the manual labor involved on a working farm. But a few days at a time is enough, and back he goes to his next dancing job.

John Kriza is always looking forward to the next role, the next adventure, and to whatever fun may be around. With a twinkle in his alert gray eyes, he says: "If I could live my life all over again, I'd live it exactly the same way!"

Hugh Laing

H UGH LAING was a full-grown young man when he saw his first
ballet. That one performance changed the course of his life
instantly and forever.

Hugh had only recently arrived in London—a darkly handsome, impressionable youth of nineteen, fresh from a leisurely,
provincial life in far-off Barbados. It was on that serene and beautiful tropical island of the West Indies that he was born, of English
and Irish parents. Nothing in his life there had prepared him for
the wonders of London. He haunted the art galleries, and began
to study painting. He went avidly to the theaters and considered
becoming an actor. Then one night he happened to go to Marie
Rambert's famous Ballet Club at the tiny Mercury Theatre.

Hugh sat transfixed through the whole evening. That performance was a revelation—ballet was the most beautiful thing he
had ever seen. Here were the drama and the painting that he loved.
And here was more—an exquisite combination of music and movement. He made an instantaneous decision—he was going to be a
dancer, no matter how late a start he had and no matter how long
it took! He promptly enrolled as a beginning student in Mme
Rambert's ballet school.

From the first day he stood tentatively at the *barre*, his lessons
were enormously satisfying. Mme Rambert was just the kind of
teacher that energetic, imaginative Hugh needed. In her school
and theater Hugh met stimulating companions, some of whom became lifetime friends—Alicia Markova, and two choreographers
doing their early work: Frederick Ashton and Antony Tudor.

Hugh knew what he wanted right from the start. The classical
ballets were not for him. He felt drawn instantly to the modern
ballets Ashton and Tudor were creating—ballets in which acting
was just as important as dancing.

HUGH LAING in *Pillar of Fire*

Though he was prepared to go slowly, Laing forged ahead so quickly that he danced his first solo role after less than two years of training. Of that role as the Prince, in one of Tudor's first ballets, *Atalanta of the East,* he says now in his direct, animated way: "Naturally I was terrified, but actually I've been much more terrified in later roles. In that first solo, I still hadn't learned what great responsibility you carry in a lead."

He stayed with Rambert's Ballet Club for four years, studying and performing with increasing preoccupation. Occasionally he went to Paris to take lessons with the great Russian teacher, Olga Preobrajenska. In 1935 he began lessons with Margaret Craske in London, and has studied periodically with her ever since.

As early as 1937, a collaboration began that was to last for years—Laing and Tudor. The two of them with their friend, Agnes de Mille, formed Dance Theatre in London, and went on together the following year in The London Ballet. These two close friends came to America in 1939 to join Ballet Theatre at its inception.

Ballet Theatre was launched at Center Theatre in Rockefeller Center in January 1940. Laing shared his first American success with his friend, Antony Tudor, because *Jardin aux Lilas,* in which he made his debut, was the first Tudor ballet to be seen in America.

Two other ballets, given *premières* in 1942, made Laing the most talked-about *premier danseur* in Ballet Theatre. The roles themselves were as different as night and day. The first, by Antony Tudor, was *Pillar of Fire, premièred* at the Metropolitan in April. Laing's performance as the subtly brutal Young Man from the House Opposite was a perfect foil for Nora Kaye's Hagar, and established him as a master of dramatic dancing.

In October of that same year he danced his second unforgettable role. In Massine's *Aleko,* which boasted a distinguished cast (Markova, Skibine, Tudor, and Hightower), Laing's flashing, virile dancing as The Young Gypsy was a sensation.

Laing danced The Young Gypsy all over the United States, but of all those dozens of performances, one has become almost a legend—which Laing delights in recounting. He and Markova were dancing in *Aleko* on the huge outdoor stage of Hollywood Bowl when suddenly she fainted dead away—so gracefully that it seemed a part of the ballet. Laing, always cool-headed, never stopped dancing. He swooped down to gather the unconscious ballerina in his arms, and, improvising as he went, danced offstage and deposited her carefully in the wings. Another dancer hastily put on a duplicate of Markova's costume and joined Laing on the stage. Muriel Bentley, the heroine of the occasion, had never danced Markova's role, but Hugh, by means of rapid, whispered instructions, guided her adroitly through the final minutes of the ballet. So smooth was the substitution that the audience was not even aware that Markova had fainted.

Back in New York in 1944, Laing met an attractive newcomer to the cast—tall, curly-haired Diana Adams. They first danced together in *Undertow* the following year, and two years later they were married. In 1950, after Laing had been dancing with Ballet Theatre for ten years, the two of them joined the New York City Ballet, in which they are both stars today.

Laing is emphatic in his belief that it is much better for a dancer to be married than not, especially if he is married to another dancer. "If I come home tired out, Diana understands, and if she comes home tired out, I understand. It's wonderful."

They live in a midtown New York apartment, where Laing carries on a hobby rather unusual for a city-dweller: carpentry. His electric saw is a permanent fixture in their large living-room, and with it and a few hand-tools he has constructed most of their simple, modern furniture. On the walls are several of Hugh's own modern oil portraits and paintings.

His life as a dancer is a satisfying one, and he wakes to each new day full of good spirits and anticipation for the role he is to dance that night. His current favorite is *Prodigal Son*. The ballets that typify Laing for most audiences are the modern, complex works of Antony Tudor. These great ballets have given Laing his most satisfying means of expression, and his superb pantomimic dancing has added distinction to every one of them.

Tanaquil LeClercq

"**D**ANCER YESTERDAY, BALLERINA TODAY**"** ran a headline on the theater page of *The New York Times* of February 28, 1952. On the previous night, said the story, young Tanaquil Le-Clercq of the New York City Ballet had danced the Swan Queen in *Swan Lake* for the first time, replacing Maria Tallchief. She had given a superb interpretation, in spite of almost paralyzing fright, and had won her official recognition as a ballerina. Long-legged, freckle-faced Tanaquil LeClercq, just twenty-two, that night became the youngest ballerina of the country's leading ballet company.

Tanaquil had been working toward that night for fourteen long years, and had given up many of girlhood's pleasures to attain it. She was born in Paris in 1929, the daughter of a Frenchman, Jacques LeClercq, a professor of literature, and the former Edith Whittemore, a St. Louis society woman, and a thwarted ballet dancer. Tanny, as she has always been called, came to New York with her parents when she was three, and almost immediately was enrolled at the progressive King-Coit School, where dancing was a regular part of the curriculum. Tanny, at four, danced the role of a swan in the school's ballet *Nala and Damayanti*.

From the time she entered the Mordkin Ballet School, when she was eight, Tanny, a shy rather withdrawn child, felt far more at home in the large, barren practice-room than she did anywhere else. After two years she entered the School of American Ballet, where she showed such extraordinary promise that she soon won one of the school's five scholarships—for which she competed with 130 other applicants.

There was no doubt in anyone's mind now that Tanny was to be a dancer. Dancing took up four to five hours a day, seven days

TANAQUIL LECLERCQ in *Metamorphoses*

a week, which left little time for anything else. She couldn't fit regular school into her schedule, and had to study with a tutor.

She was still a student at the School of American Ballet when George Balanchine, its director, formed his new company, Ballet Society, in 1946, and chose her to dance a solo at the opening performance. The opening was a triumph, and sixteen-year-old Tanaquil LeClercq, dancing the role of Choleric in Balanchine's *Four Temperaments*, shared in the general acclaim.

She danced with such spirited flair that Ballet Society granted her their first fellowship so that she could continue to study at the School of American Ballet even while she was dancing with the company. Her promise as a dancer became ever more evident in *Divertimento, Highland Fling, Symphonie Concertante,* and in her first really important solo as Ariadne in *The Minotaur.* Shortly afterward, when she danced the second movement of Balanchine's *Symphony in C* with Francisco Moncion, critic Anatole Chujoy wrote: "LeClercq danced with the ease, fluidity and technical brilliance that the audience is growing accustomed to expect from this young dancer."

By 1948, she was officially a soloist with the company. When, late in that year, Ballet Society was reorganized as the New York City Ballet, Tanny was one of the new company's principal dancers. New York audiences, proudly enthusiastic over its new company, grew to wait eagerly for the appearance of the tall, lanky, rather coltish young dancer with the unpronounceable name. In the smash-hit *Orpheus,* she danced the role of Bacchante; in *Illuminations* she was Sacred Love—two widely divergent roles that showed off her remarkable adaptability. She was lyric in *Symphonie Concertante,* romantic in *La Valse,* and showed a bitter, frantic gaiety in *Lilac Garden* as The Woman in His Past.

It is impossible to type LeClercq as a dancer, for she changes with each changing role. Her long, flexible, reed-thin body can appear angular and brittle, as it does in *Metamorphoses,* or soft and fluid as in *La Valse.* Her face is just as mobile. Even her eyes change from gray-green to gray-blue, depending on what she wears, and her whole face, which seems almost plain one moment, flashes to real beauty the next.

Although long-legged Tanny is 5-feet-6, her energetic life and high-strung nerves keep her weight at little more than one hundred pounds. She eats little, admitting that she is too nervous to eat before a performance, and too exhausted afterwards. She relaxes best with her favorite hobby, photography, and likes to develop and enlarge her own pictures. She "loves" movies, "loathes" sports, and on vacation heads for "any place that is warm" where she can "lie around and do nothing."

Tanaquil LeClercq is matter-of-fact about her profession. Ballet dancing is her job, she says, and she is glad to be good at it, because she couldn't do anything else even if she wanted to. Like any job, it has its disadvantages, the biggest ones to her being the inadequate salary and the shortness of a dancer's professional life.

In the fourteen years of training that made her a ballerina, one man guided her all along the way—George Balanchine. LeClercq might almost be called a Balanchine product, for all of her study and professional experience have been in organizations that he directs, and her greatest successes have been in roles that he created especially for her. Their close and inspired association reached its culmination on New Year's Eve of 1952, when Tanaquil LeClercq became Mrs. George Balanchine.

David Lichine

THE London theater is packed to overflowing, with a fashionable audience come to see the famous French company, Les Ballets des Champs-Élysées. The *première* of David Lichine's new ballet, *La Création,* is about to begin.

There is no music at all as the curtain goes up. The stage is completely bare of scenery. A heap of bodies lies motionless on the floor. In the center of the stage sits The Choreographer (Jean Babilée) with his head in his hands, despairing. He is in the throes of creating a new ballet, and is agonized because the idea that he needs will not come. From the pile of bodies he picks up a leg here, an arm there—but he cannot bring them to life. In desperation, he picks up a limp body (Leslie Caron), but he cannot make it dance, because he does not really know what he wants it to do. Suddenly The Idea (Tatiana Riabouchinska) comes to him and everything begins to move at last. The bodies slowly come to life, and one by one The Choreographer leads them in the steps that are to be his ballet. Just at the moment when the real creation starts, the curtain goes down.

Before the ballet was half over that night, David Lichine, its creator, rushed from the theater to wander the streets in torment. He was sure that his strange, abstract ballet, into which he had put his whole heart, would not be a success. The audience was bound to think he had done the ballet without music or scenery just for effect, and would dismiss it as pure sensationalism. Lichine himself knew that the ballet had to be done starkly—it was the only way.

For hours after the performance, he could not bring himself to go back to the theater. Finally he heard that for the full nineteen minutes of *La Création* there was not a sound from the audience— not even a rustle of a program. When the curtain went down there was silence for a moment, then wild, prolonged applause.

TATIANA RIABOUCHINSKA and DAVID LICHINE in *Graduation Ball*

La Création became the talk of the ballet world, and its *première* that night in 1948 remains to this day the greatest surprise and triumph of David Lichine's eventful life. The ballet has never been danced in the United States, he says regretfully, because he has not yet found a producer willing to take a chance with it.

David, the son of a musician and composer, was born in Rostov-on-Don, Russia, in 1910. Fleeing the Revolution, he went with his family first to Bulgaria and finally to Paris. As he grew up, athletics was the most important thing in his life, until, when he was seventeen, he suddenly became interested in dancing.

He enrolled for ballet classes with Mme Lubov Egorova, and was absorbed in the lessons from the very first day. "My positions were all wrong, everything was wrong, but it was wonderful!" It was just what he wanted to do. With each passing day his preoccupation with ballet grew. Dancing, he discovered, was far more vigorous and satisfying than the sports he had once thought all-important. Today Lichine says emphatically: "Ballet is the greatest sport there is."

He went on to study with Mme Nijinska, and first appeared with the Ida Rubenstein Company in Paris, where the virile dancing of this eighteen-year-old attracted immediate attention. In a remarkably short time he attained the rank of *premier danseur*. He won wider acclaim as he progressed from the Anna Pavlova Company to the Col. de Basil Original Ballet Russe (where he first danced with his future wife, Tatiana Riabouchinska) and then to the Ballet Russe de Monte Carlo. This young *premier danseur* with the sensitive, intelligent face and the dark brooding eyes seemed half-man, half-faun as he danced. The vitality and robustness of his technique set off the elusive, romantic quality of his interpretation.

A near-tragedy in 1937 abruptly halted David Lichine's career as a dancer. During the Coronation festivities for King George of England, Lichine was scheduled to dance in a command performance of *Cotillon*. He arrived so late at the theater on the night of the performance that he scarcely had time to get into his elaborate costume. Hastily he pulled on his heavy cotton stockings and, without taking time to put on his long garters, tied them tightly above his knees. His role was a very long one, and with each of his leaps and *entrechats* he could feel his legs throbbing and swelling. By the end of the performance, he was in agony because the tightly tied stockings had cut off the circulation. Blood-poisoning was the result. The doctors were not sure that David Lichine would ever dance again.

During the long years of recovery, when he could not dance, he turned entirely to choreography. Some of his best work came out of this period of enforced rest: *Francesca da Rimini, Prodigal Son,* and *Graduation Ball.* Lichine soon found, however, that it was impossible for him to do choreography without actually dancing. So he forced himself back into dancing condition. He had to get rid of the extra weight that eight years of inactivity had added to his normally lean, flexible body, and to retrain the muscles that had lost their tone and strength. In speaking of the rigid self-discipline he endured, he says: "To stop dancing is not difficult. It is to start again that is really hard."

Finally, in 1944, he was dancing again before an audience, as guest artist with Ballet Theatre. He began to tour again, both in the United States and Europe, but limited himself to short roles that would not overtax him.

Now that he was dancing again, his choreographic talents overflowed. As guest choreographer with Les Ballets des Champs-Élysées he did two of their most remarkable ballets—*La Rencontre* and *La Création,* in both of which young Leslie Caron and explosive Jean Babilée starred. Lichine briefly turned his talents to movie-making in Hollywood, where he created the ballets in several movies, the most recent being *Tonight We Sing,* in which Tamara Toumanova plays the role of Pavlova.

After several seasons during which Lichine and his wife danced together as guest artists with Ballet Theatre, they sailed in 1951 for London to appear as guest artists with Festival Ballet, for whom Lichine also created several ballets. In 1952, they danced for a few months with Ballet Theatre, then returned to France, where Lichine formed his own company, Ballet de la Ville des Anges.

David Lichine has much to say artistically, for his is an original art and an original mind. He talks with vast assurance, humor, and charm of his long years in ballet, and of his theories on choreography and the training of dancers. To illustrate one of his theories, he cites his daughter. Little Tania will not dance until she is ten because Lichine believes not only that "a child should have a childhood—a time to play with dolls," but that too-early training can definitely harm a child's muscular development. A child is ready, both muscularly and emotionally, to begin the arduous training of a dancer at the age of ten.

"Ballet uses the best muscle, the best music, and the best imagination of a country," says Lichine, who believes that in order for ballet to be fully developed as a national art it must be subsidized by the government. It is his sincerest hope that some day there will be some such permanently based, nationally subsidized ballet company in the United States, which is his adopted country and the one he calls home.

Serge Lifar

THE magnificent building that houses the Paris Opéra today stands on the very site of ballet's original home, The Royal Academy of Dancing and Music, founded by Louis XIV in 1661. For the past hundred years, the Opéra has been the citadel of ballet tradition in France, and Opéra-trained dancers have gone out from its gilded doors to dance for the world. For the past two decades, it has been directed by Russian-born Serge Lifar, its ballet master, *premier danseur*, and choreographer. He wields a tremendous influence, and it is largely because of his inspired direction of the Opéra that ballet in France today is once more vital and original.

What is he like—the man who has dominated the scene of the dance in Paris for so long? At first glance, Serge Lifar is not particularly impressive. He is of medium height, with straight black hair, penetrating gray-green eyes, and rounded Slavic features. But when he steps out from behind his desk the casual grace of his compact, muscular body reveals the dancer. When he begins to speak, one meets the full force of his striking personality. His speech reveals a keen mind, completely dedicated to his all-consuming passion, ballet. A listener can almost hear the capital letters with which he pronounces the sacred words *"Mon Art."*

Serge Lifar's preoccupation with ballet began in his native city of Kiev, where he was born in 1905. When still a boy, he was suddenly tossed into the turmoil and chaos of war—the First World War and then the Russian Revolution. He managed to complete his education and even to continue his studies of piano and violin. Interested in all the arts, he had no idea of what he wanted to do with his life until a friend took him to watch a ballet class. Enthralled with what seemed to him the perfect combination of all the arts, he enrolled at the Studio Centrale d'État in Kiev to study with Mme Bronislava Nijinska.

He had been at the school for only one month when Mme Nijinska left to join the Diaghilev Ballets Russes in Paris as choreographer and ballet mistress. Young Serge continued his lessons, and several years later Mme Nijinska wrote from Paris, requesting that five of her favorite pupils be allowed to join her in the Diaghilev Ballet. Permission was granted by the school and the government, and Serge, one of the five, started out eagerly with his comrades. The trip across the heavily guarded Russian border was a nightmare, and it was a frightened eighteen-year-old who finally reached the haven of Paris and the Diaghilev Ballets Russes.

Serge was somewhat crestfallen to discover that he was not to be allowed to dance in performances with the company, but was put to work instead with the *corps de ballet* in their daily technical classes. Determined to improve his position, he gained permission to spend his holidays the following summer studying with the great maestro Enrico Cecchetti at Turin. On his return to Monte Carlo weeks later, he had made such noticeable progress that everyone remarked on it.

His reward was his first appearance on stage with the *corps de ballet* in *Sleeping Beauty* and *Les Noces*. Rapidly he rose to the position of soloist, becoming a *premier danseur* in 1925. The next four years added immeasurably to his stature as a dancer. In 1929, Diaghilev gave him his first chance to try his hand at choreography —a revival of *Le Renard*, which was presented shortly before the close of that brilliant season.

Serge's bright hopes of the future plummeted to despair when on August 19, 1929, the unbelievable word went out to all the members of the company that impresario Serge Diaghilev was dead in Venice. After some months of uncertainty and deep depression, Lifar was summoned to the Paris Opéra. Young choreographer George Balanchine had been working on a revival of the ballet *Prométhée,* but had fallen ill. Lifar stepped in and finished it. Both his choreography and his dancing in the ballet were so outstanding that they resulted in his immediate appointment as *premier danseur* and ballet master of the Opéra.

SERGE LIFAR in *David Triomphant* with YVETTE CHAUVIRÉ

This position was an unusually important one for a young man of twenty-five, and during the next fourteen years Lifar became the Opéra's guiding light. At the peak of his prestige, he appeared also as guest artist with the Ballet Russe de Monte Carlo, where his brilliant dancing as the Prince in *Giselle* and in the *Blue Bird pas de deux* remains unforgettable to this day.

In 1944, as the result of a political squabble, Lifar left the Opéra to join the Nouveau Ballet de Monte Carlo. But three years later he was back again at the Opéra as *premier danseur*, ballet master, and chief choreographer. He has held this many-faceted position ever since.

He has had a series of sensational successes at the Opéra: *Icare, David Triomphant* (with Mia Slavenska) and *Alexandre le Grand* (in which Yvette Chauviré danced opposite him) were the earliest. Among his most recent ballets are *Blanche Neige, Four-*

beries, and a satire on Hollywood, *Cinema, premièred* in 1953. For each of these ballets, Lifar was not only choreographer-dancer, but also the creator of the musical rhythms.

Ballet is Serge Lifar's single passion. In order to keep up with his heavy responsibilities at the Opéra, he follows a rigid pattern of hard work which excludes almost any personal life. He spends his mornings in study and meditation, working on the manuscript for his latest ballet book (he has published almost a dozen). He devotes his afternoons to choreography, rehearsing his dancers and directing the activities of the school. He goes to every performance at the Opéra, whether he is dancing or not, and frequently sits up half the night in conference with his dancers. Sometimes he interrupts his afternoon activities to take important visitors through his renowned ballet library. This huge collection, said to be the largest and most complete in the world, consists of rare manuscripts, books, mementos, and photos—a priceless treasury of ballet lore. Many of these he has collected himself, during the years of his devotion to ballet, and others are continually being sent him by interested collectors all over the world.

Lifar, who has been called one of the most brilliant products of Diaghilev's regime, has, like Diaghilev, been the guiding force in the lives of the young dancers who come under his influence. Yvette Chauviré, now listed by many critics as one of the four top-ranking ballerinas in the world today, was the first of Lifar's discoveries. So certain was he of her potentialities that he created several ballets especially to show her off: *Le Roi Nu,* in which she danced the role of the Queen, *Alexandre le Grand,* in which she danced the Jewess, and *Blanche Neige.* Another of his protégées is Renée Jeanmaire. Still another is Jean Babilée, now *premier danseur étoile* at the Opéra. Youngest of Lifar's discoveries is beautiful, promising Liane Daydé, the baby of the Opéra.

For Serge Lifar, who finds that "only in ballet do I fulfill myself entirely," the future offers a rich and colorful vista, because for him there will always be "a new ballet, a new book, and always especially a new discovery!"

Colette Marchand

COLETTE MARCHAND, a striking girl with chestnut hair and flashing black eyes, has already won fame on two continents—as a dancer in ballet and musicals, and as an actress in her first movie, *Moulin Rouge.*

One of her most remarkable qualities is her chameleon-like ability to change her whole appearance and personality. She herself says: "I am one thing one day, and something absolutely different the next." Watch her dance in *L'Œuf à la Coque*—she is a sophisticated temptress, saucy and earthy. Watch her, on another night, dance her favorite classical ballet, *Swan Lake*—this time she is as fragile and remote as a moonbeam. Then see her in her first acting role in *Moulin Rouge*, where as Marie Charlet she is a bawdy spitfire. In each role, Colette is completely different and completely convincing.

But, in speaking of her glamorous career, Colette says intensely, groping in her still-unsure English for just the right word: "I detest my life as a dancer! It is *terrible*—the hardest life in the world. I have no time for diversions, no time for friends." Then the snapping black eyes soften unexpectedly as she adds: "But I keep on with it, nevertheless!"

She was born in the French province of Brittany in 1925. Her father, a manufacturer of electrical equipment, had practical plans for his little daughter, which were to include a college education. But when Colette showed an inclination to dance, and her mother encouraged her, he was talked into letting her be enrolled at the Paris Opéra Ballet School. She began in the traditional way when she was eleven, as a *petit rat*, appearing in Opéra productions as a flower, an angel, a fairy. When she was fourteen, Colette was elevated to the *corps de ballet* of the regular Opéra Company.

Now Serge Lifar, ballet master and director of the Opéra,

began to watch young Colette carefully. He tried her out in his own ballets, *Le Chevalier et la Damoiselle* and *Sylvia*. She was hailed as a new Lifar discovery, and critics spoke highly of her dancing, but Colette herself felt that things were going far too slowly. She began to put on small performances of her own, in which she danced the leading roles. When she was twenty-two, and no further along at the Opéra, she went to London, where she was promptly made the leading ballerina of England's newly organized Metropolitan Ballet. She was delighted to be starring, at last, in such classical roles as the Queen in *Swan Lake* and as Juliet in *Romeo and Juliet*.

From here on, Colette's life began to assume the hectic pace that stimulates and at times infuriates her. She was swept into Roland Petit's Ballets de Paris, and made a name for herself with her highly provocative dancing in *Les Demoiselles de la Nuit*. Going on to London with the company, she created an even greater stir with her racy *L'Œuf à la Coque*. Both of these ballets were later greeted with unrestrained approval in New York, where press agents promptly dubbed sleek Colette "Les Legs"—a name which still follows her today, much to her chagrin.

Colette remained in New York at the end of the company's engagement, first as guest artist with Ballet Theatre, then as a featured dancer in Bert Lahr's musical, *Two on the Aisle,* in 1951.

Meanwhile, talent scouts had spotted "Les Legs" and lured her to Hollywood with a six-month contract at one of the major studios. True to tradition, she cooled her heels for the entire six months, with nothing to do. At the end of this frustrating period, she returned to Paris.

Colette appeared briefly as a ballerina with Anton Dolin's Festival Ballet, then turned once more to the field of the music hall. Ironically enough, it was while she was dancing in Maurice Chevalier's revue, *Plein Feu* ("Full of Fire") that Hollywood "discovered" the girl who had been ignored on their own doorstep the year before. Director John Huston, in search of a French girl to play the part of Marie Charlet in *Moulin Rouge,* opposite José

COLETTE MARCHAND
in *Swan Lake*

Ferrer, knew he had found her the minute he set eyes on Colette. In spite of her protests that she had never acted, and knew practically no English, Huston later remarked that she was one of the finest natural actresses he had ever seen. *Moulin Rouge* won a fistful of Academy Awards—and Colette Marchand, who was called a "whirlwind of quick-changing emotions," won her unquestioned place as a first-rate actress.

She went back to ballet as Roland Petit's leading lady when he reorganized his Ballet de Paris in 1953. But she has no intention of limiting her diverse talents to any one medium. Movies, music hall, ballet—capricious Colette sees her future in them all.

Alicia Markova

I<small>F THE</small> brilliant career of Alicia Markova were beginning today, it is likely she would use the plain English name with which she was christened—Alice Marks. But when she began to dance in the early 1920's, only the Russians had prestige as dancers, and audiences would have been amused, if not actually affronted, had the name of an English girl appeared on the program of the great Diaghilev Ballets Russes.

The last thirty years have seen the emergence of ballet schools and companies in many nations, and dancers are proud to use the names that label them the products of their own country's training. Today there is no need for a Fonteyn to become a Fontenova, or for Nora Kaye (born with the good Russian name of Koreff) to hide her American birth behind a misleading name.

The name that tiny Alice Marks adopted when she joined the Diaghilev Company at the age of fourteen has become a glittering symbol of all that is beautiful in ballet. Alicia Markova is, and has been for many years, a dancer of such perfection that she has often been called the greatest classical ballerina in the world. Now, at an age when many dancers begin to think of retirement, Markova is still queen of the ballet world.

She was born in a London suburb in 1910, of an English engineer father and an Irish mother. A long series of illnesses left her pale, undersized, and scrawny, and when she was nine her doctor suggested ballet lessons as a last resort.

Little Alice, who had never seen dancing of any kind, was firmly marched to Miss Thorne's Dancing Academy in London. She was pleased almost at once with her lessons because, she says serenely today: "I was better than the other children in the class, and could do things they could not do." It was instantly apparent that this child, frail as she was, was destined for greatness. When

ALICIA MARKOVA as *Giselle*

she was ten, she made a real professional debut as the leading dancer in a Christmas pageant, which brought her floods of publicity, with enthusiastic references to her as "The Child Pavlova."

Quite carried away by her small daughter's success, Alice's mother had cards printed reading "The Miniature Pavlova," and took her child to the studio of Mme Seraphima Astafieva, the first great Russian teacher to open a school in London. Mme Astafieva took one look at the card, one look at the pint-sized child, and flew into a furious tirade. All mothers were alike, she stormed! Just because their offspring could "stand on one toe and wobble," they were all Pavlovas. She slammed the door in their faces.

Alice's mother, considerably chastened, finally persuaded Astafieva to watch her child dance, after which she was promptly admitted as a student. The shy little girl made friends almost at once with a young English lad, Patrick Healey-Kay, who years later, under the name of Anton Dolin, was to be her greatest partner. Dolin couldn't help liking the well-behaved little girl, but claims that "she annoyed me, as much as she did the other pupils, with the unbelievable ease with which she could do anything!"

After Alice had been working with Mme Astafieva for four years, her father died, and it was up to her, the eldest daughter, to support her impoverished mother and three sisters. Hastily, her mother decided that Alice must go into vaudeville, but before this dire decision could be acted upon, Serge Diaghilev, who had seen her working at Astafieva's studio, providently asked her to join his company. For Diaghilev, who had a lifelong aversion to child dancers, this was an unheard-of step!

Fourteen-year-old Alice, a slight child with black hair cut in a Dutch bob, arrived in Monte Carlo, accompanied by a strict governess and her mother and bearing her newly-Russianized name of Alicia Markova. She spoke no Russian, and most of the dancers spoke no English, but she nevertheless began shyly to make friends. Alexandra Danilova, who was next in age to Alicia, and had been with the company only three months herself, remembers: "One day at rehearsal they bring me a little dark girl, very

The Sugar Plum Fairy in
The Nutcracker

thin, very tiny, and I try to be kind to her—for it is not nice to be new in a company." Alicia herself says: "Danilova was kind to me in many ways. Knowing that I loved chocolates, and that my governess wouldn't allow me any, Danilova would bring some to rehearsals in the morning, saying: 'But if you no dance well, I bring you no more!'"

Diaghilev watched over his little English dancer with extreme care, putting her to work with Mme Cecchetti, one of the best Italian teachers for children. The first role that she danced was Little Red Riding Hood in *The Sleeping Princess*. Next she danced a small excerpt from *Swan Lake*. Then, when she created the role of the Nightingale in George Balanchine's ballet *Le Rossignol*, she caused such a stir that a less wise man than Diaghilev might have been tempted to push her to stardom at once. But Diaghilev, who was a stickler for thoroughness, said to the child: "I want you to learn everything you can about every phase of ballet as you go." Markova has never forgotten those words. As a result of his patient insistence, she gained a thorough knowledge of music, décor, lighting, and costume—in addition to the complete choreography of every ballet she danced. Today, people speak almost in awe of her ability to remember every detail of choreography. She herself says: "I like to know the whole ballet. I don't see how anyone can know what she is doing unless the whole work is part of her."

Alicia danced with the Diaghilev Company for five years, touring Germany, France, and England. When she was nineteen, just before the season in which she was scheduled to dance her first leading role, Diaghilev died. It is reported that in his last press interview he said: "Watch my little English girl."

Alicia Markova's career was abruptly halted, for at the time of his death she was still almost unknown except to a handful of balletomanes. She remained in Monte Carlo disconsolately for a while, then returned to England. There was no established ballet company in England at this time, so Alicia took whatever commercial engagements she could find—at London music halls and movie houses—often with Anton Dolin as her partner. Dolin drily comments on this early partnership: "To the dismay of the highbrows, we were an enormous success!"

In 1930, Alicia joined Marie Rambert's struggling new Ballet Club, where young Antony Tudor doubled as stage manager and choreographer, Hugh Laing was just beginning his career as a dancer, and Frederick Ashton was doing his early choreography. The dancers performed on a tiny stage in a converted church on Sunday evenings, and were paid just enough to cover bus fare and toe-shoes. Markova, remembering those early days when she was first a ballerina, says: "That was the beginning of my adaptability. When they say to me now 'Madison Square Garden' or 'television,' I am not worried. I know I can dance anywhere, having gone from Diaghilev's magnificent productions in the great opera houses of the world to Ballet Club's tiny hall, where one was almost in the audience's laps and had only a piano for accompaniment!"

For some years, Alicia made her living dancing commercially, and satisfied her artistic instincts at the Ballet Club and the Camargo Society. Early in 1933 she was taken on as a ballerina with the Vic-Wells Ballet, and her appearances so bolstered the box office that later in the year she was named *prima ballerina* of the young company. Full-length versions of all the great classics were revived to show off the brilliance of this tiny, airy ballerina, and London audiences packed the little theater to see the English girl who outdanced the Russians in *Swan Lake, The Nutcracker,* and *Giselle.*

After a year, during which the company prospered as no English company had prospered before, Markova left to form a company of her own with Anton Dolin—the Markova-Dolin Ballet. "All my life," she says now, "I shall form new companies, moving on from those which do not need me, giving work to more young dancers." The Markova-Dolin Ballet, with its dazzling stars, was immensely popular for the two years of its existence.

Markova's impact on American audiences, who first saw her in 1938 with the Ballet Russe de Monte Carlo, was stunning. Her New York debut in *Giselle,* with Serge Lifar, brought the whole city and its press to her feet. Audiences called her dancing incredible and magnificent, and critics referred to her as the greatest classical ballerina in the world. She was inevitably compared to the legendary Anna Pavlova. Markova even looked like her, with her heart-shaped face, limpid dark eyes set against petal-pale skin, and glossy black hair. She was said to dance like her, with the same unbelievable lightness and ineffable charm.

Prima ballerina Markova, in the years since America first saw her, has whirled from one company to another, from one unbelievable triumph to another. She was with Ballet Theatre from 1941 to 1945, and since then has been guest star with companies all over the world: Original Ballet Russe, Sadler's Wells Ballet, and smaller companies from South Africa to South America. Periodically, she has reestablished her partnership with Anton Dolin. They revived the Markova-Dolin Company for an American tour in 1947, and danced together again a few years later in Dolin's Festival Ballet. In 1953, the eternally lovely Markova added luster to England's coronation festivities as guest artist with Sadler's Wells Ballet.

"I can't understand people who speak of being bored!" Markova says in her light, small voice. "There are not enough hours in the day to accommodate all of my interests." Markova, who has been described as anything from "a goddess" to "a nice-looking English girl," dresses beautifully, for clothes are her one real extravagance. Still underweight, she needs eight hours sleep, plus an afternoon nap, many cups of tea, and frequent light meals to keep her weight at ninety-eight pounds. She is just 5-feet-2, and though she looks delicate enough to snap at a finger's pressure, the strength that underlies her dancing is phenomenal.

Markova's fame alone is enough to fill any theater in which she appears. No matter what she dances—whether the purely classical *Blue Bird pas de deux* or the starkly modern *Rouge et Noir* —audiences adore and applaud her. Her gypsy Zemphira in *Aleko* is just as perfect as her Princess Aurora; her Can-Can as delightful as her Swan Queen. But being essentially a classical ballerina, she loves one role above all others, and it is the one that has brought her the greatest fame—the title role in *Giselle*. In fact, her sister says: "Sometimes we think she *is* Giselle!"

The ultimate in tributes was paid Markova by John Martin, critic of *The New York Times*, who wrote a few years ago: "She is not only the best living ballet dancer, but probably the greatest who has ever lived." After this accolade had appeared in print, Agnes de Mille, one of Markova's closest friends, reports that she asked her how it felt to read such a statement about herself. Miss de Mille says that Markova replied: "It's easy to write something like that, but it's I who have to live up to it. What am I going to do the next day, I ask you? I must work all the harder. The audience is going to expect something after reading that bit. It will be hard lines if I let them down!"

But audiences and critics, both in the United States and Europe, have learned to expect perfection of Alicia Markova, and they always get it. "It is as though the air were her element, as though no effort were involved in the most difficult of technical feats," one critic wrote. "Markova is the miracle that never fails."

Mary Ellen Moylan

FROM the day she first thought of being a dancer, Mary Ellen Moylan was plagued by the plain Irish name with which she had been christened. Who had ever heard of a ballet dancer with a prosaic name like Mary Ellen? She changed it tentatively a couple of times, but on the eve of her first tour to Europe as a ballerina the question of her name was settled once and for all.

Alexandra Danilova, the most illustrious star of the Ballet Russe de Monte Carlo, cornered pretty hazel-eyed Mary Ellen on the night before the company sailed. "Little one, we must do something about your name! You simply cannot dance in Europe with three names!" she announced. But the young ballerina protested, laughing, that it was too late. Her name was already quite well known, and she was finally beginning to rather like it herself! So she went to Europe with three names, and the name that she refused to change is today known over much of the world—the simple Irish name of Mary Ellen Moylan.

Mary Ellen was born in Cincinnati in 1926, and began lessons in tap and acrobatic dancing when she was a tyke of three. Five years later, after the family had moved to St. Petersburg, Florida, she had her first real ballet lessons.

The unforgettable summer when she was eleven, her mother took her talented little daughter to New York for a month's study at the School of American Ballet. After those wonderful weeks, the little girl knew that what she wanted more than anything else was to be a ballet dancer. Back home again, she decided earnestly that the first thing she must do was change her name to something more romantic. Out of the blue, she picked "Mimi," and refused to answer to anything else. By the time the next summer rolled around, "Mimi" Moylan was back for another month's study at the School of American Ballet. Crushed to discover that her new name only made people laugh, she went back to being just plain Mary Ellen once more.

At the end of that second blissful summer she won a scholarship at the school, and her mother allowed her to remain in New York and live with her aunt. For the next three years, she scarcely knew that any world existed outside of the school. She arrived every day even before the janitor, and sat patiently on the steps, knitting and waiting for the doors to open. She devoted every spare minute to practice, working ten hours a day, and would gladly have forgotten all about regular school studies if her aunt had not insisted that she study at night with a tutor. "I learned to study on the run, and I'm still doing it!" Mary Ellen says today.

She signed her first contract when she was sixteen, as *première danseuse* with the New Opera Company in New York. She made her debut in the leading dancing role in *Rosalinda*, and was offered another leading role at the same time—in George Balanchine's new *Ballet Imperial*. For several breathless weeks, Mary Ellen managed to dance two different roles in two different theaters simultaneously. Each night, after dancing her role in *Ballet Imperial* at the Broadway Theater, she dashed from the wings to her dressing-room, made a lightning change to her *Rosalinda* costume, hailed a taxi for a cross-town dash, and arrived backstage at the other theater just in time for her cue!

The first week of *Ballet Imperial,* her name appeared on the program simply as "Mary Ellen." When critics referred to her as "Miss Ellen" the young dancer found it far too Victorian for her liking. The next week's program carried her name once more as Mary Ellen Moylan.

After ten months with *Rosalinda,* seventeen-year-old Mary Ellen joined the Ballet Russe de Monte Carlo as a soloist. She danced roles of increasing importance in the next two years, in *Snow Maiden, Serenade, Les Sylphides,* and *Le Bourgeois Gentilhomme.*

She left the Ballet Russe de Monte Carlo to dance in two musical comedies: *The Day Before Spring* and *The Chocolate*

MARY ELLEN MOYLAN and **OLEG TUPINE** in *pas de deux* from *The Nutcracker*

Soldier. But two years on Broadway were enough—Mary Ellen was homesick for ballet.

In 1947, she was back with the Ballet Russe de Monte Carlo as a full-fledged ballerina. She began to be increasingly teamed with handsome *premier danseur* Oleg Tupine, whose height and broad shoulders were such a perfect foil for her own tall, slim grace that their fellow dancers took to calling them "the greyhounds of the Ballet Russe." The lyric perfection of their *pas de deux* from *The Nutcracker*, and the tenderness with which they danced *Swan Lake*, sent critics searching for adjectives to do Moylan justice: brilliant, beautiful, polished, they called her. This dark-haired Irish colleen, they remarked, was turning into a dancer of true distinction.

Mary Ellen Moylan is a regal beauty on the stage, and an extraordinarily pretty and appealing young woman off it. Very feminine and very chic, she likes all the things a pretty girl should like: parties, beaux, and clothes. She is enthusiastic about her hobbies: collecting earrings, reading, and painting, and was very pleased when some of her little sketches recently appeared in *Dance* magazine. But she would give up anything, without a moment's hesitation, that threatened to interfere with her dancing.

She joined Ballet Theatre in 1950 for its European tour, starring in *Helen of Troy*, the *Black Swan pas de deux*, and *Theme and Variations*. As one of the company's top ballerinas, she glitters in almost every classic work in its repertoire. Recently, in *Les Demoiselles de la Nuit*, and in the title role of *Princess Aurora*, Moylan has shown a warm and brilliant maturity that has captivated audiences everywhere. Critic Anatole Chujoy has summed it up: "Awareness, sincerity, musicality, line, figure, technique—Moylan possesses them all in full measure."

Nina Novak

O N THE fateful night that the first German bombs fell on Poland
in 1939, young Nina Novak, one of Poland's most promising
dancers, was appearing in the Opera House in Warsaw. Two days
later the Opera House was destroyed by bombs and Nina's world
collapsed around her.

Though her whole life had been devoted to ballet, Nina now
had no heart for dancing. But the invading Germans decreed that
anyone who did not have a job of his own would be conscripted for
work camps. At considerable risk to her own safety, she refused to
dance at the large theater that the Germans had taken over, and
joined a group of Polish dancers in a tiny, ill-equipped theater,
giving performances only for their own countrymen.

The dark years of World War II wore on. One by one, the
members of Nina's large and wealthy family were arrested, and
sent to concentration camps—first, her adored older brother, then
her father, and then Nina herself, along with her brothers and
sisters. They were separated and scattered to different camps, and
Nina frantically asked for news of her family from each new prisoner who came to her camp. Dreary months dragged by before the
tragic news got through to her—her beloved brother had been
killed for anti-Nazi activities. Her father, too, was dead—of starva-
tion.

Dazed with grief, Nina no longer cared whether she lived or
died. By the time liberating troops arrived six months later, and
threw open the prison gates, Nina was so emaciated that she could
scarcely walk.

Hardly comprehending that the war was over, she listlessly
began to pick up the threads of her life. She was reunited with
what was left of her family, and as they attempted to make some
sort of life for themselves in devastated Poland she felt the vague

stirrings of the old familiar desire to dance. But she was still too dispirited and weak to practice. Her younger brother, to encourage her, began to practice with her, and before long they had built up a charming little dance routine of their own. Together they found dancing engagements in various Warsaw nightspots. The family unanimously decided that the only hope for Nina as a dancer lay in the United States, so little by little they put aside enough money for her to make the long trip.

Nina arrived in New York in 1947—a slight girl whose tragic dark eyes held the only hint of the heartbreak she had been through. She set about learning to speak English, and started intensive ballet lessons to retrain her still-frail body. She applied for a position in the *corps de ballet* of the Ballet Russe de Monte Carlo in 1948, and was accepted. She worked furiously, determined to rise to the top. Four years later, she had made the grade—as top-ranking ballerina with the Ballet Russe de Monte Carlo.

"When I want to do something, I want to do it one hundred per cent!" says Nina Novak with uncompromising intensity. The goal on which her whole being has been focused ever since she was seven years old has been to be a really great ballerina no matter what the cost.

Her first schoolteacher in Warsaw, where she was born, noticed little Nina's natural grace and told her she should study dancing. Nina delightedly reported her teacher's words at home, only to be met by her mother's firm reply that no daughter of hers was going to be a dancer! But Nina, a determined child, coaxed and raged until her mother reluctantly allowed her to enroll at the Polish Opera Ballet School.

Her first real appearance on stage came three years later, when she was allowed to dance the part of a slave girl in the opera *Aïda*. Shortly after this night, Nina became a real professional, dancing for two years as "*Prima Ballerina* of the Children's Ballet" of Warsaw.

She was taken into the Polish Opera Company itself when she was thirteen, the youngest dancer ever to become a member of its

NINA NOVAK and LEON DANIELIAN in the *Black Swan pas de deux*

corps de ballet. The following year, Nina started out with the company on a long European tour. Those two stimulating years, dancing in the capitals of Europe, saw Nina rise from her humble position in the *corps de ballet* to soloist, winning roles of increasing importance.

She had scarcely returned to Warsaw after this tour, when the Polish State Ballet was invited to dance at the World's Fair in New York early in 1939. But while she was dancing lightheartedly in New York, the clouds of war were darkening over her native country. Nina had been home for only a month when Hitler marched into Poland.

In spite of the bitter war, which brought her heartbreak and physical collapse, Nina says today: "Always in life I have luck— I *really* have luck!" She insists it was luck that brought her two of her greatest roles. The first was Swanhilda in *Coppélia*, which Nina danced on three days' notice when the Ballet Russe de Monte Carlo was in Chicago. She replaced Danilova, who was ill, and danced with such effervescent spirit that she got rave notices from the Chicago critics.

It was luck again, according to Nina, that brought her the role with which she is most closely identified, in *Mute Wife*. The ballerina who had been rehearsing the leading role had a temperamental clash with the choreographer, and walked off in a huff. "So who was there?" asks Nina, smiling reminiscently. "Little Nina!" *Mute Wife* has been her own notable role ever since.

She has won a leading role in almost every ballet in the repertoire of the Ballet Russe de Monte Carlo. Still driven by ambition, she is so completely dedicated to her profession that nothing else matters to her. Nina Novak has taken for her creed the words of her teacher of long ago: "If people tell you that you cannot dance, do not believe them, for you can. But if they say that you are wonderful, do not believe them either, for you must always improve."

Roland Petit

IN THE midst of the sprawling, noisy produce district of Paris called Les Halles stood a small, all-night café—Chez Petit—a popular rendezvous for tourists and nighthawks. Chez Petit boasted two "specialties of the house": one of them the onion soup and the other a tousle-haired, high-spirited little boy, the son of the proprietor, who danced and clowned around the restaurant in a pair of ballet slippers several sizes too big for him. The patrons, delighted with his nightly antics, threw him coins, which he scooped up with a slightly mocking bow. "What is your name, little boy?" they asked again and again. With a proud toss of his black curls, the boy replied: "My name is Roland Petit."

Today, everyone in Paris knows the name of the young dynamo who is Roland Petit, for he is famous as a brilliantly gifted dancer, choreographer, and founder of two ballet companies. His fame has spread to England, Africa, and America, where his companies have toured. Millions of other Americans saw Petit for the first time in the movie *Hans Christian Andersen*, in which his dancing with Jeanmaire was so spirited that Hollywood press agents were inspired to advertise Petit as "the man who put sex in ballet"!

Everything Roland Petit does is colored by his unfailing originality and his impatience with tradition—two traits that were apparent even when he was a small boy. He was born in Villemomble, a suburb of Paris, on January 13, 1924—the son of a French father and of an Italian mother from whom he gets his crisp black curls and darkly flashing eyes. From the day his mother brought him a pair of ballet slippers from the dress shop where she worked, Roland's feet were never still. He made up new dances every day, and tried them out every night on the customers at the restaurant. His father, afraid at first that his patrons would be annoyed, soon found that his son's dancing was actually bringing in new customers.

By the time the lad was ten, his parents decided they had better send him to the Opéra Ballet School, to see what they could do with this young whirlwind in action.

Roland proved to be a brilliant, charming, often exasperating student. "Oh, I was a crazy child!" he says himself. He fretted at the slow, tedious process of becoming a ballet dancer, but worked with lightning speed so that he could be through with the whole thing and dance in his own way. He vowed that when he grew up he would do ballets such as Paris had never seen! Until that day, he would learn all that the school could teach him.

He joined the *corps de ballet* at the Opéra when he was sixteen. Two short years later, he did the choreography for his first ballet, *Paul and Virginia*. Although at the time people said that it was a surprisingly original piece for an eighteen-year-old, the ballets he has created since are so strikingly unconventional that they make that first effort seem trite by comparison.

Roland quit the Opéra Ballet when he was twenty-one. He was so infected with the holiday mood of just-liberated Paris that he couldn't wait any longer to strike out on his own. Now was the perfect time to make a beginning! Carefully, that December of 1944, he picked a dozen youngsters, some of whom were former Opéra Ballet students, and set about organizing his Galas de Danse —a series of Friday night performances of his own ballets. They were instant hits. Paris wildly applauded these young unknowns: Petit, his fiery and provocative partner Renée Jeanmaire, Jean Babilée, Colette Marchand, Nina Vyroubova, and the others.

The unexpected success of these ten performances was all it took to set Roland Petit on fire to form his own permanent company. But he needed money. He went to his father at Chez Petit and persuaded him to borrow money on his little café. With this loan and the help of Boris Kochno, a well-known figure in Paris theatrical circles, Petit formed Les Ballets des Champs-Élysées in 1945. He took along his dancers from the Galas, and later added a young unknown—fifteen-year-old Leslie Caron.

The *première* of Les Ballets des Champs-Élysées in October

ROLAND PETIT in *Carmen*

1945 was a triumph. With each new performance, Parisians flocked in increasing numbers to see this young company. They applauded with equal enthusiasm the ballets by Roland Petit himself and the classical stand-bys: *Swan Lake, Blue Bird,* and *Spectre de la Rose.* His *Les Amours de Jupiter* (March 1946) was enormously successful. Within a few months, when volatile Jean Babilée starred in Petit's *Le Jeune Homme et la Mort,* the company had a sensational hit on its hands.

From the night of the 1948 London *première* of the extraordinary ballet *La Création,* Les Ballets des Champs-Élysées became the talk of the Continent. Roland Petit was creating a vital new ballet form, using the best modern dance techniques applied to a thoroughly classical foundation. His company was an inspired combination of youth, originality, fine artistic collaboration, and superb dancing, welded into unity by Petit himself.

After two highly successful seasons in both Paris and London, Petit sent his Ballets des Champs-Élysées on tour to Egypt, and later to South America. He himself stayed behind in Paris, where he organized another company, Les Ballets de Paris. He continued creating and producing his own special brand of ballets, among them a free-form version of Bizet's *Carmen*. Petit and Jeanmaire, as the ill-fated lovers, danced daring love scenes that startled and delighted audiences in Paris, and later in London, where *Carmen* played to packed houses for a full season. On the heels of their London success, Petit took Les Ballets de Paris to America, where for a full four-month period in 1949 *Carmen* played to Standing Room Only in New York's Winter Garden.

Hollywood caught up with Petit the next year, when he returned for a second American tour. He was hired as choreographer and dancer for Samuel Goldwyn's production of *Hans Christian Andersen*. Although Petit says the ballets he created for that movie were "a bit too classical" for his taste, movie-goers found them exciting and novel.

Restless as always, Petit left the United States after the highly publicized New York *première* of *Hans Christian Andersen*. He returned to Paris, bursting with impressions of Hollywood, which he immediately transcribed into two satirical ballets. In March 1953 he opened his reorganized Ballets de Paris at the Empire Theatre with ravishing Colette Marchand as his leading lady.

The impression he left behind in America is a vivid one. Everyone who met him speaks of his colorful personality, engaging humor, and agile mind, which seems to spout ideas in all directions at once. Yet they feel he is a contradiction, too. Although "bored" with classical ballets, he spends two hours a day going through the disciplined, traditional ballet work-outs. And although he is impatient with "people who talk ballet, ballet, ballet all the time," he himself talks ballet constantly—the ballet of Roland Petit.

Janet Reed

JANET REED is often asked what it's like, dancing up there on the stage. By way of answer, she tells of the time she danced her first big role, as Swanhilda in *Coppélia*.

At that time, Janet, a pretty, redheaded teen-ager, was a member of the San Francisco Opera Ballet. During the weeks of rehearsal on the stage of the Opera House, the asbestos curtain had never been raised, and Janet was accustomed to the snug feeling of dancing with the curtain down. On opening night, as the first strains of the music for *Coppélia* drifted backstage, she nervously took her place. Slowly the curtain went up, and Janet, completely alone on stage, gazed across the footlights at the tremendous, shadowy cavern of the Opera House for the first time. "I've never been so frightened in my life," she recalls. "The vast sea of faces stretched away into the darkness farther than I could see—strange faces looking at me with opera glasses. I felt so tiny and lost." Panic seized her, and as she moved through the first slow steps her muscles seemed frozen. She cast an agonized glance into the wings, and her eye caught a familiar figure, the stage director. Nodding his head happily, he was looking at her as though she were the most wonderful thing in toe-shoes that had ever been on the stage of the Opera House. "That did it," Janet remembers. "I forgot the audience, forgot the opera glasses, forgot myself—and just danced!"

That night was Janet Reed's first and only experience with real stage-fright. Audiences, she soon discovered, were nothing to be frightened of, especially San Francisco audiences, who adored their tiny ballerina.

San Franciscans claimed her as their own discovery, and Janet herself felt that the "City by the Golden Gate" was home, even though Oregon was her native state. Born in Tolo, a hamlet boasting, then as now, a population of fifteen families, she moved to Portland when she was eight, and began ballet lessons.

Deciding at sixteen that she wanted to devote all her time to ballet, Janet enrolled in the Portland school of Willam Christensen. Shortly afterwards, when Christensen moved to San Francisco, where he had established another school, he took his best pupils with him—among them Janet Reed. And when he became choreographer and artistic director of the San Francisco Opera Ballet in 1937, Janet went along as a member of the *corps de ballet*. This pert, charming redhead became a great local favorite and, beginning with that first performance of *Coppélia* in 1939, was the star of the Opera Ballet. When she danced in the first American full-length version of *Swan Lake,* San Francisco ballet-goers fairly burst with pride.

It was a real loss to the West Coast ballet scene when Janet left it in 1941 to join Dance Players in New York. She herself was fascinated with this new experimental group. "Dance Players was a rewarding experience because I was constantly doing new things," she says. "But as happens to a lot of progressive ideas, the group was an artistic success and a commercial failure."

Dance Players folded after a year. Janet spent the next three years dancing as ballerina with Ballet Theatre, touring the States and Canada. She scored her first widespread success with the *première* of *Fancy Free*, in the role of one of the Passers-By picked up by the exuberant sailors. Her warm, delicate personality and sprightly dancing charmed her audiences, as well as the critics. The following year came her second big success, *On Stage!*, in which her dancing of the appealing, stage-frightened Little Girl in Pink caused one critic to write with unabashed enthusiasm: "She's a darling!"

By the time Janet Reed left Ballet Theatre in 1946, she had a whole series of roles to her credit: Mexican Sweetheart in *Billy the Kid*, the Wife in *Tally-Ho*, the French Ballerina in *Gala Performance*, Youngest Sister in *Pillar of Fire*, Competition Girl in *Graduation Ball*.

"My best things have been purely American," says blue-eyed Janet, who prefers modern ballet to anything else. This love of

JANET REED in *Cakewalk*

Americana led her to try her luck in a Broadway musical in 1948, as the leading dancer in *Look, Ma, I'm Dancing!* When the show closed, after a very successful run, Janet went back with Ballet Theatre for a season. In 1949 she joined the New York City Ballet, where today, dancing in her favorite ballet, *Pied Piper*, she still manages to look like a fourteen-year-old.

Offstage, Janet is a friendly young woman, full of warm enthusiasm about dancing, about life in general, and especially about her family. In private life she is Mrs. Branson Erskine and the mother of a son, Reed. She says, with utter sincerity: "My first concern is with my family and home, and to do a good job of raising my child. Dancing must now take second place." Her affiliation with the New York City Ballet is ideal, she says, for she can spend almost all her time with her family.

When the company left on an extended tour of Europe in 1952, Janet's husband and son went along. Her husband combed the European market for antiques for his Madison Avenue shop. He and Janet, who have always been fond of French cooking, delighted in adding to their collection of exotic herbs and recipes. For young Reed, the whole tour was high adventure, especially the first night he watched his mother dance in Spain. After the performance the audience put on a typical Latin demonstration that the whole company is still talking about. Cheering wildly, they turned loose a flock of white doves in the hall and flung flowers on the stage until the smiling dancers were knee-deep in them. In telling of this ovation (which the Spanish call a "homage") Janet adds with a charming touch of practicality: "Of course, flowers are cheaper in Spain than they are in New York."

The dancers were much moved by this Spanish demonstration, for though they had been received enthusiastically everywhere, there had never been anything to equal this. It added a touch of glamour that, Janet says, is all too lacking in a ballet career today. With a twinkle in her bright blue eyes she adds: "No one comes backstage any more bearing diamond necklaces, but that homage made us all feel like queens!"

Tatiana Riabouchinska

THERE is nothing lovelier than April in Monte Carlo, when the whole countryside is abloom. But inside the dark Monte Carlo theater, that April of 1932, spring was forgotten. The dancers were rehearsing day and night, driven by the relentless energy of Leonide Massine, because the *première* of his new ballet, *Jeux d'Enfants*, was only a few hectic days away.

David Lichine was to dance the leading role of the Traveler, but as yet no one knew who would be chosen for the coveted role of the Child. Every night, blonde, elfin Tatiana Riabouchinska, who was just fourteen, dreamed that she would be chosen to dance with the romantic young *premier danseur*. But during the day, working earnestly and tirelessly through long hours of practice, she did not dare hope that this prize would really be hers. After one especially discouraging and exhausting day, as she drooped dispiritedly against the wall, ballet master Massine suddenly pointed a commanding finger at her. "You, Tania! You will dance the Child!"

And so it was—at the *première* of *Jeux d'Enfants* on April 14, 1932, with the De Basil Ballet Russe, that Tania danced for the first time with her future husband, David Lichine.

"That was where it all began," Tatiana Riabouchinska says today in her soft, sweet voice. But her story really began in Moscow, where she was born in 1918. Her mother, who had been a dancer until her marriage to a wealthy Moscow merchant, began to instill in her two little daughters a love for the great traditions of ballet. Tania was too young to remember when her family fled from their luxurious home during the Revolution and made their difficult way to Paris. There Tania and her older sister grew up in considerable luxury, quite unlike the existence that less fortunate refugees suffered. Tania was a delicate child, with straight fair hair, wide blue eyes, and a sweetly elusive charm. When she was ten her mother, concerned at her delicacy, decided to start her at ballet lessons, which she hoped would build up her child's strength and would also open up to her the whole world of the arts.

At the end of her first year's study with Mme Olga Preobrajenska, she appeared in a recital to which all the Paris critics had been invited. Tania's small solo—a variation on a dance by Pavlova led one enthusiastic critic to write: "Watch Tatiana Riabouchinska. That girl will be something!" This prophecy was soon to be fulfilled.

Tania made her professional debut when she was twelve, with the Chauve-Souris. Then in 1932, fame beckoned her. Col. de Basil, who had reorganized his Ballet Russe de Monte Carlo, decided to gamble everything on three unknown dancers, all mere children, whom he billed as "The Baby Ballerinas." Tatiana Riabouchinska, who was fourteen, was one. Tamara Toumanova and Irina Baronova, both thirteen, were the others. People came in droves to the glittering *première* in Monte Carlo, curious to see these much-publicized youngsters. They were astonished to discover that these girls were not only pretty and charming, but were remarkable dancers, and the evening ended in a riot of applause for them.

Everywhere they toured, the Baby Ballerinas created a delighted furor. But De Basil found it almost impossible to meet the overwhelming expenses of touring. His large troupe, composed primarily of under-age dancers, had the additional burden of twenty-four mothers who traveled with their children. As the company went on through the capitals of Europe, he was never quite sure that he could hold it together financially.

Things looked bleak by the time they reached London in July 1933 and gave their first performance at the Alhambra Theatre. But London gave them a reception that far surpassed anything they had anticipated, and the theater was sold out night after night. De Basil's worries were over, and The Baby Ballerinas became the toast of London.

Tatiana Riabouchinska's dancing was much admired during

TATIANA RIABOUCHINSKA and ADOLPH BOLM in *Carnaval*

that whole season—which stands out, even today, as one of the
brightest in ballet history. Tania whirled from one role to the next,
showing a new facet of her remarkable talent with each new role:
Prelude in *Les Sylphides*, Columbine in *Carnaval*, Frivolity in *Les
Présages*, the Dancer in *Petrouchka*, and the Golden Cockerel in

Le Coq d'Or. In all these roles, Tania showed the gay elfin charm that still captivates her audiences today.

The wild success of the London season was echoed in New York, where the company made its debut in December of the same year. All over the United States, the much publicized Baby Ballerinas were greeted with enthusiastic acclaim, often playing a matinee in one town and an evening performance in another to satisfy the demand. Tania remembers the next ten years as just one tour after another—back and forth across America and back and forth to Europe.

During most of these years, Tania and David Lichine danced together with the Ballet Russe de Monte Carlo. After his serious injury in England, they were separated for a time. But in 1942, they were reunited in Hollywood, where Tania was on tour and Lichine was making a movie. They were married that same year— just ten years after they had danced together the first time. As husband and wife, the Lichines have been guest artists with Ballet Theatre, Les Ballets des Champs-Élysées, and the Festival Ballet. Now they dance together in France in Lichine's own company. But no matter where their careers take them, Hollywood is their home, and it was there that their little daughter, Tania, was born in 1946.

Little Tania looks like the child of dancers—very slim, very straight, very much the little water-sprite. She has her mother's thick dark-blonde hair and sweetly serious look, and her father's eyes, dark and fathomless. Although she will not start ballet lessons until she is ten, little Tania dances all over their hilltop house, running on her toes. As her mother fondly watches, she says in her sweet, low voice: "I did not believe it when my mother told me I used to run on my toes, but now I see my own daughter doing the same thing!"

Just as Tatiana Riabouchinska's mother passed on to her a love of ballet, so Tatiana herself is passing on to her own little daughter this same heritage. It seems extremely likely that the story of Tatiana Riabouchinska will have its sequel in the yet unwritten story of little Tania Lichine.

Moira Shearer

IN A crowded London bus some years ago, a delicate red-haired young girl sat unobtrusively darning a pair of ballet slippers. They had to be finished before she arrived at the Sadler's Wells Ballet School. Presently a courtly little old man sat down next to her and, after watching in attentive silence for a few minutes, spoke of his own interest in dancing. Then he took a silver thimble from his pocket and presented it to the girl, saying: "Keep this for luck, my dear," and was gone before she could even thank him.

Moira Shearer has kept that silver thimble as a good-luck piece ever since. Though she has no idea who the old man was, she firmly believes that the thimble he gave her that day, when she was just a student, still brings her luck now that she is a star. Her mother wears it, at Moira's insistence, every time her daughter dances a new role.

Moira Shearer King was born in Dunfermline, Scotland, in 1926. At the age of six she went with her parents to Rhodesia, where her father, a civil engineer, was temporarily stationed. In that unlikely place, Moira had the surprising luck to find a ballet teacher who had once danced in the Diaghilev Company, and it was with her that she began her studies.

The King family returned to Scotland when Moira was eight. She saw her first real ballet shortly after, when her parents took her to London to see Leonide Massine dance in *Boutique Fantasque*. It was a tremendously exciting evening for the little girl, but Moira admits today that she was more interested in the audience and the gleaming jewels and elegant evening gowns than she was in the dancing. The full significance of that evening was not realized until twelve years later when, at the same theater, at another performance of *Boutique Fantasque*, the little girl who had been in the audience that night was the partner of Leonide Massine.

When Moira was ten, Nicholas Legat, the most sought-after teacher in London, consented to take her as a pupil. Her eager and inquiring mind drank in everything he taught her, and her imagination was stirred by all she saw and heard in his famous studio. She worked with Legat for three years, until his death, and then went on studying with his wife.

Moira entered the Sadler's Wells Ballet School when she was thirteen. Inevitably she began to dream of the day she would be suddenly called from the school to the Sadler's Wells Theatre itself, to be a Snowflake in *The Nutcracker* or one of the Mice in *Sleeping Beauty*. But she had been a student scarcely two months before war broke out, and the school and theater were shortly closed.

The months that followed were miserable ones for Moira. Back home in Scotland, she doggedly practiced alone, but knew she was getting nowhere. In the midst of her deepest discouragement she received a letter from the International Ballet, asking her to join them on tour. Moira joyfully hurried back to London to rehearse. She danced her first small solo with so much confidence that it was called "the most successful single dance of the evening." She toured England with the company for a year, and in spite of blackouts, air-raids, and dozens of wartime difficulties she felt she was living at last.

When the Sadler's Wells reopened in its wartime home, Moira went back as fast as she could get there, becoming a full-time student once more. Her career slowly began to take shape, though there were times when this self-critical young dancer felt that the great roles she longed for were hopelessly beyond her reach.

She was taken into the regular company in 1942, dancing small solos in *Sleeping Beauty*, *Coppélia*, and *Les Sylphides*. Two years later, she substituted for Margot Fonteyn as Odile in the ballroom scene of *Swan Lake*. The audience caught its breath as Moira Shearer made her dramatic entrance that night in her black and gold dress, with her burnished hair gleaming. She was radiantly beautiful and had a vast assurance that carried her superbly through the role.

MOIRA SHEARER in the motion picture *The Story of Three Loves*

Her recognition as a dancer of true distinction began in 1946, when Sadler's Wells moved into its new home at the Royal Opera House, Covent Garden. In that year, nineteen-year-old Moira danced principal roles in four great ballets: *Sleeping Beauty, Symphonic Variations, Coppélia* and, finally, in the full-length *Swan Lake.* Critics praised her dramatic quality and her magnificently fluid style. They called her "the discovery of the year."

Now she began to receive tempting movie offers—but Moira turned them down, one after another. She would not allow anything to interrupt her progress as a dancer. Even when she was first approached about a movie to be called *The Red Shoes,* she firmly said no. After almost a year of persuasion, she finally agreed to dance in the movie, largely because she would have the stimulation of working with two great dancers: Leonide Massine and Robert Helpmann.

With the release of *The Red Shoes* in 1948, Moira found with dismay that she was a movie celebrity. Reporters and photographers besieged her Kensington home, and her telephone rang so incessantly that it had to be disconnected. To escape this glare of publicity, for which she had no taste, she went into hiding until the worst of it had died down. But, even then, offers for movie contracts continued to come in. Moira, ignoring them, quietly went back to class and rehearsal at Sadler's Wells.

She was asked so repeatedly to explain her puzzling attitude that she finally gave the newspapers a statement, which read in part: "If I seriously thought of accepting any of the contracts, it would mean finishing any further career as a dancer, which I certainly have no intention of doing. The ballet means far too much to me."

Reserved British balletomanes worried lest Moira's sudden fame affect her dancing. But when in each new role she danced—in *Giselle, Don Juan, Cinderella*—she showed a more mature brilliance, they sighed with relief. One critic paid her the ultimate in compliments when he wrote: "She has surmounted the handicap of her movie fan appeal."

With Sadler's Wells's first trip to the United States in 1949, her dancing and her bright beauty dazzled audiences everywhere. Back in England the following year, Moira married novelist Ludovic Kennedy, and moved into a little antique-filled white house in Knightsbridge. Then came the second tour to the United States in 1950, which carried the company all the way across the country. Moira's husband was with her on this trip, and thoroughly enjoyed the adulation that his wife received everywhere.

Moira Shearer was now a star of the first magnitude. It was an event of almost national interest when she dropped out of the company for a few months in 1952 to have her first baby. The British public, avidly interested in everything she does, approved wholeheartedly when she revised her original decision and made two more movies: *Tales of Hoffmann* and *Story of Three Loves*. They note with interest the fact that she has been taking dramatic lessons with the avowed ambition of becoming a good enough actress to act in Shaw's plays. But level-headed Moira Shearer says: "There is plenty of time. Meanwhile, all my thoughts lie in perfecting myself as a dancer."

George Skibine

GEORGE SKIBINE had his life all mapped out the summer he was seventeen. He was going to be a mechanical engineer, and was all set to start his studies the following fall. Meanwhile, he landed a summer job as a chorus boy at a Paris café. By the time school began, the field of electromechanics had lost a potential genius. Handsome, Russian-born George was sold on being a dancer.

George had been surrounded by dancing and talk of dancing from the time he was born in 1920, because both of his parents were dancers: his Russian father a ballet dancer, and his Belgian mother a modern dancer. His father joined the Diaghilev Ballets Russes in Monte Carlo when George was a small school-aged boy. From then on, George divided each year between winters in Paris at a Jesuit boarding-school and summers in Monte Carlo with his father. Everyone automatically assumed that young George, too, would become a dancer. No one was more surprised than his father when his teen-aged son announced, one summer, that he'd decided to be an engineer! But he had reckoned without his heritage. When he found himself dancing at the Bal Tabarin, he realized suddenly that dancing was more satisfying to him than anything else could be.

The kind of dancing he wanted was ballet. To begin his training, he picked one of the best teachers in Paris, Mme Olga Preobrajenska. He kept on with his job at the Bal Tabarin to pay for his lessons, which soon became the most important thing in the world to him. After several months of study, he began to dance with the Ballets de la Jeunesse. George was now one of the busiest young men in Paris—lessons every morning with Mme Preobrajenska, rehearsals every afternoon at both the Bal Tabarin and the Ballets de la Jeunesse, and evening performances that sometimes doubled

GEORGE SKIBINE with ALICIA MARKOVA in *Aleko*

up on him, sending him panting from the ballet to the night club.

At the end of his first year of ballet training, eighteen-year-old George returned to Monte Carlo as a professional dancer, a member of René Blum's Ballet de Monte Carlo. He has a vivid recollection of his first solo, as the Deer in *Seventh Symphony*, because he very nearly had to dance it without a costume. In the frenzy of preparations for the *première*, costume designer Christian Bérard somehow completely overlooked the Deer. Just before dress rehearsal, on the morning of the *première*, George went looking for his costume. There wasn't one! All that day the Deer stood patiently in Bérard's workshop while the designer and his assistant, busy with a thousand details of the dress rehearsal, frantically cut and pinned a costume for him among their other chores. George arrived at the theater only minutes before his cue, sewn up in his costume and completely exhausted. "But strength seemed to come back to me before I went out on the stage," he recalls, with a smile lighting his earnest blue eyes, "and I danced the role full out."

At nineteen, he joined Col. de Basil's Ballet Russe de Monte Carlo, and a year later was off with them on a tour to Australia, where he began to dance his first *premier danseur* roles.

Ballet Theatre, home of many of the most promising young dancers of the day, asked him to join the company as *premier danseur* in 1941. With his very first American appearance, this tall, strikingly dramatic young man, who danced with such virility and spirit, made an instant impression. New York critics commented enthusiastically on his performances in *Swan Lake, Princess Aurora,* and *La Fille Mal Gardée.* Then, when he danced Prince Sapphire in *Bluebeard,* critics began to rave. "Skibine," they said, "danced with such personal radiance that he lifted the ballet to new heights of romance." A particularly flowery tribute in *The New York Times* led directly to what George wryly calls "the most unforgettable experience of my dancing career," when Sol Hurok, the company's impresario and manager, after reading this press notice, promptly doubled Skibine's salary!

The furor over George Skibine reached a new climax with the

première of Ballet Theatre's *Aleko* in 1942. This ballet, the story of a young Russian, Aleko, who leaves his home to follow his gypsy sweetheart, only to lose her to a gypsy rival, starred Skibine as Aleko, Alicia Markova as Zemphira, and Hugh Laing as the Young Gypsy. Audiences went wild, and critics were not far behind. *Aleko* and George Skibine have been inseparable in the minds of ballet-lovers ever since. Years after opening night, they were still comparing every new Aleko with Skibine's. George Skibine, they said nostalgically, danced Aleko with a restrained intensity and a haunting tenderness that were never equaled after he left the company.

At the end of 1942, having just become an American citizen, George Skibine enlisted in the U. S. Army and was promptly shipped to France as a sergeant with Counter-Intelligence. With the First Army, he participated in the D-Day landing in Normandy, a duty for which he was extraordinarily well equipped, having intimate knowledge both of the language and the countryside. All that he will admit about those years however, is that they taught him "a bit" about guns and shooting, which are still his most engrossing hobbies. He has won several medals as a sharpshooter, and likes nothing better than a Saturday of target practice.

Ex-Sergeant Skibine joined Massine's Ballet Highlights with ex-Seaman First Class Youskevitch for the summer of 1946. The fall found him dancing with the Original Ballet Russe, where he met a brown-haired, flashing-eyed ballerina, Marjorie Tallchief. These two young dancers were soon dancing together, and in George's own words: "Marjorie and I danced into such smooth performances that we seemed a natural team." They were married in 1947, and immediately afterwards joined the De Cuevas Grand Ballet, where George was promptly established as top-ranking *premier danseur*.

George Skibine's modesty and sincerity remain unchanged. His honest technique, his extraordinary emotional range, and his winning personality have established him with critics and public alike as one of the most admired dancers of the day.

Mia Slavenska

PEOPLE who think of ballerinas as fragile, impractical beings have reckoned without Mia Slavenska. This dynamic Yugoslav is not only an outstanding ballerina but an efficient businesswoman who has organized and directed three ballet companies of her own with conspicuous success.

She starred in her dual role of ballerina-businesswoman on the cross-country tour of her Ballet Variant in 1948. The company traveled in a specially designed bus, in which Mia had had the regular seats replaced by comfortable swivel-chairs. Amiable Dr. Kurt Neumann, Mia's husband and manager, drove, and in the seat next to him was Mia herself, chic in a voluminous tweed coat, with her bright red-gold hair tied back in a small peruke. Between them in a basket their infant daughter slept contentedly.

Arriving in each new town, Mia was off like a shot to the theater, auditorium, or school—wherever they were to appear that night. She spent the whole day directing operations: supervising the scenery, arguing with musicians and stage managers, munching a sandwich at lunchtime, putting the cast through a dress rehearsal. Every once in a while, her husband would say coaxingly: "Mia! Sit down, here by me. You can direct things just as well sitting down!" But Mia never did. Those who watched her exhausting activity all day marveled when they saw her dance that night. Her performance was as vigorous and fresh as though she had done nothing all day. When the rest of the company wandered wearily back to the hotel and bed, Mia, still full of bounce, often dragged her uncomplaining husband off to a local nightspot for a little expert jitterbugging.

This energy of Slavenska's, which gets her through her usual ten- to fourteen-hour working day, has also carried her through a startling variety of achievements. She was born in Yugoslavia, the

MIA SLAVENSKA in the *Black Swan pas de deux*

daughter of a poor druggist. Her theater-struck parents, who were frustrated actors, took their infant daughter to every show in near-by Zagreb. From the first, Mia says, there was never any doubt in her own mind that some day she would be on the other side of the footlights.

When she was four, her mother enrolled her at the ballet school of the Zagreb National Opera, and a year later she was a child star in Opera ballets. She danced throughout Yugoslavia on a concert tour when she was barely twelve, and was something of a national figure by the time she was in her early teens.

She joined the *corps de ballet* of the Ballet Russe de Monte Carlo in 1934. Four years later, having carried off one of the three international prizes at the Berlin Dance Olympics in 1936, Mia returned to the Ballet Russe de Monte Carlo as a full-fledged ballerina. Although Danilova and Markova were the great stars of the company, young Slavenska often alternated roles with them. When she went with the company on its first tour of the United States, audiences were carried away by her vitality and vivid personal magnetism. Her moving performances in *Swan Lake, Coppélia,* and *Le Baiser de la Fée,* and the warm, earthy quality of her dancing in *Gaité Parisienne* won her "bravos" of approval.

Mia was just as enthusiastic about America as it was about her. After she co-starred with Yvette Chauviré in the movie *Ballerina,* she returned to the States, and has been in a whirlwind series of activities ever since. She formed her first small company in 1944; danced in the musical *Song Without Words;* taught ballet in Hollywood; and began to do choreography too. In 1948, she formed her second company and, after its eventful tour, joined the Ballet Russe de Monte Carlo as guest artist. She founded her third company in 1952—the Slavenska-Franklin Ballet.

With its co-directors and stars, Slavenska and dynamic Frederic Franklin, the new company had an extra attraction in its guest artist, Alexandra Danilova. Its 1953 tour of the United States and Japan added another success-filled chapter to the story of irrepressible Mia Slavenska.

Maria Tallchief

To SEE Maria Tallchief, top ballerina with the New York City Ballet, dance is to see brilliance and fire that few other dancers can equal. Her compelling magnetism, her flashing *pirouettes* and fast, precise movements are so exciting that critic John Martin was moved to say: "Tallchief can not only accomplish the impossible, but she dances the incredible!"

The Maria backstage is quite another sort of being. The fires are banked behind a dreamy, languid manner as she sits before her make-up table, accenting her soft brown eyes with mascara and combing her luxuriant, straight dark hair. She speaks softly and quietly, in her velvet voice, almost as though she were dreaming aloud. There is an aloofness and an all-enveloping serenity about her, and one feels that only on the stage does she come completely and dazzlingly alive.

She was born Elizabeth Marie Tallchief in 1925 in Fairfax, Oklahoma. The fact that her father, Alexander Tallchief, is an Osage Indian and that Fairfax is a community within an Indian reservation makes Maria careful always to point out that her family home was a house and not a tepee!

She has early memories of watching Indian tribal dances, and of making up little dances of her own—sometimes allowing her adoring younger sister Marjorie (now a ballerina with the De Cuevas Grand Ballet) to dance with her. When a visiting teacher began to give piano and dancing lessons in the community, little Maria showed a startling aptitude in both.

Her parents, sensing real talent in their daughter, moved to Los Angeles when Maria was eight to put her in the hands of expert teachers. She started piano lessons at once, and was simultaneously enrolled with Ernest Belcher, one of the best dancing teachers on the West Coast, with whom she studied "stage dancing"—acrobatic, Spanish, tap, and ballet. Her dancing, however, was never allowed to interfere with her piano lessons, for it was by now decided that Maria was to be a concert pianist.

Little Maria's daily schedule, by the time she was ten, would have worn out an adult. Up at six-thirty every morning, she practiced the piano for an hour before going to school. She took a piano lesson every day from three to four o'clock, after which she went on to her ballet lesson at five.

From the time she was twelve, and began to study ballet with Bronislava Nijinska, the brilliant Russian teacher, Maria was torn between her two interests. She was a pianist of such ability that she gave frequent recitals when she was in high school, often playing as guest pianist with small symphony societies around Los Angeles. Her dancing, too, was bringing her enthusiastic notice, and she appeared in regular dance recitals. At fourteen, she gave a whole evening's recital, dancing half the program and playing the piano the other half. Remembering those hectic days, Maria sighs: "I was an honor student in grade school, but in high school something had to suffer, and I'm afraid it was my formal studies."

The tide turned completely in favor of ballet after she appeared in Hollywood Bowl in 1940, dancing a solo in Nijinska's ballet *Chopin Concerto*. The huge audience might have disconcerted even a veteran dancer, but Maria danced with composure, remembering: "I was more dazed than nervous. I was just fifteen at the time. Nerves come later!"

Maria was taken into the *corps de ballet* of the Ballet Russe de Monte Carlo the same year that she was graduated from high school, and made her debut with them in Canada in 1942. When she first appeared with the company in New York, she was instantly recognized as an important newcomer: "one of the season's real discoveries in the classic field." In a company predominantly Russian, young Maria proudly bore her Indian name, although there were those at the time who openly wondered why she did not change it to Tallchieva!

Her remarkable talents soon singled her out for an occasional

MARIA TALLCHIEF and FRANCISCO MONCION in *Firebird*

solo—a mark of favor that caused stirrings of jealousy within the company. It is reported that one famous ballerina refused to dance with her in *Chopin Concerto* on the grounds that she was still technically in the *corps de ballet!* But she was given increasingly important solos: in *Danses Concertantes* and *Le Bourgeois Gentilhomme* in 1944, and a leading role in George Balanchine's *Night Shadow* in 1946—a role in which she stood out as an astonishing performer.

She and George Balanchine were married that same year and, although the marriage ended a few years later, Tallchief still names him as the strongest influence on her career. Several of her most successful roles are said to have been created by him especially to show her amazing virtuosity.

The venerable Paris Opéra invited her to appear for the 1947 season as guest artist, at the same time that Balanchine was guest choreographer. That year she joined Ballet Society, which, with her husband as artistic director, became the New York City Ballet. In that company, Tallchief has been the top classical ballerina.

The applause for Tallchief has increased with each passing season. When she danced in *Symphonie Concertante*, one critic wrote: "Miss Tallchief's dancing, with its air of almost savage aristocracy, and its flashing brilliance of execution, was a joy to behold." When she danced the *Black Swan pas de deux*, her performance was called a "tremendous stylistic achievement." The acclaim reached an even higher peak with her appearance in Balanchine's new version of *Firebird:* "She is so sure, strong and brilliant that it is doubtful if her superior as a technician exists anywhere today."

When the New York City Ballet appeared in London's Covent Garden in the summer of 1950, Tallchief's dancing, especially in *Firebird, Serenade,* and *Orpheus,* was greeted with flattering enthusiasm. Later that same year she scored a great success in the *Sylvia pas de deux*, and in the next fourteen months starred in four new Balanchine ballets: *Pas de Trois, Capriccio Brillant, A la Française,* and *Caracole.* In this whole series of dazzling performances Tallchief was called "a miracle of classic brilliance."

Tallchief, like most dancers, has had her share of minor mishaps on stage. There was the time, for example, that she and André Eglevsky were dancing a classical *pas de deux* in a theater in Washington, D. C. Right in the middle of it, the stagehands accidentally rang down the curtain. Eglevsky was abruptly stranded behind the curtain, with Tallchief left out in front with the audience! Eglevsky calmly walked out to join her and "we took our bows and called the whole thing finished!"

Tallchief is now married to a private-airplane pilot, Elmourza Natiroff, whom she describes as "tall, dark and handsome." In a press interview shortly before her marriage in 1952, she told newspapermen that she hopes to raise a family. "Babies are very important. That's why most people get married, isn't it?" But she has no intention of giving up her career.

With the beginning of the 1953 season, critics noticed that Maria Tallchief's technical brilliance was lighted with a new warmth that she had never shown before. John Martin of *The New York Times* wrote: "When a dancer arrives at Miss Tallchief's level of accomplishment, it is slightly foolish to talk about 'improvement,' for she has long been impeccable in style and with few, if any, peers in virtuosity. This season, however, she has clearly moved into a new phase, and one finds oneself thinking of her only secondarily as a dancer and primarily **as an artist.**" Tallchief has won her place among ballet's greats.

MARIA TALLCHIEF in *Sylvia:*
pas de deux

Marjorie Tallchief

Marjorie Tallchief plays two full-time, real-life roles: one as ballerina with the De Cuevas Grand Ballet, and the other as wife and mother of twin baby boys. Her husband is George Skibine, the leading *premier danseur* of the De Cuevas Grand Ballet, but the real stars of this gifted family are their small sons, Alexander and George, born in 1952.

Marjorie was born in Oklahoma in 1927, the daughter of Alexander Tallchief, an Osage Indian, and younger sister of Maria Tallchief. When Marjorie was six and Maria eight, the family moved to Los Angeles, where Maria was promptly enrolled in ballet school. Marjorie set up such a clamor at being left behind that to keep peace in the family she was finally allowed to go to ballet class too.

The sisters had four years of instruction with Ernest Belcher, after which they went to the Hollywood school of Mme Bronislava Nijinska for more intensive training. These two dark-haired, spirited little girls danced together at the Sacramento State Fair in 1938, their first appearance together, and their last. When the time came for them to begin their careers, they went their separate ways, Maria to the Ballet Russe de Monte Carlo in 1942 and Marjorie, two years later, to Ballet Theatre. "So we've never danced together on the stage," Marjorie says ruefully in her soft voice, "which is too bad, because I'm very fond of my sister."

Seventeen-year-old Marjorie set off on her first tour with Ballet Theatre in 1944 with a heart full of excitement. In the company of such stars as Markova, Dolin, Toumanova, and Eglevsky, she toured America and Canada for a year. In Montreal, Marjorie graduated from the *corps de ballet* to her first role as soloist—Competition Girl in David Lichine's *Graduation Ball*. Back in the United States the following year, she won her first ballerina role—Queen of the Wilis in *Giselle*.

MARJORIE TALLCHIEF in *Night Shadow* with GEORGE SKIBINE

She felt like a veteran trouper by the following year, when she joined the Original Ballet Russe. Her extensive tour of the United States with them included a grueling series of one-night stands that cured Marjorie forever of any desire to travel. Today, she speaks of touring as the one distasteful aspect of her career and mentions almost wistfully her longing for a "really permanent home."

That year with the Original Ballet Russe holds a special place in Marjorie's heart, for it was then that handsome, soft-spoken, young George Skibine joined the company. George was attracted almost at once to the tall, slender young ballerina with the wealth of shining brown hair and the warm olive skin. Before many months had passed, George and Marjorie were married.

Shortly afterwards, at the invitation of the Marquis de Cuevas, they joined his newly organized Grand Ballet, and danced at the gala Monte Carlo opening in the spring of 1947. This young husband-and-wife team is extremely popular with Continental audiences. They dance together in a variety of roles: the classical *Don Quixote pas de deux*, George Balanchine's haunting *Night Shadow*, and Skibine's own ballets, *Annabel Lee* and *The Prisoner in the Caucasus*. Marjorie's dark beauty and spirited dancing are the perfect complements to her husband's handsomeness and dash.

After the birth of their twin sons on July 3, 1952, Marjorie retired for six months. But, fascinating as her chubby babies were, she missed the familiar exhilaration of dancing. She began to dance occasional roles again. Before long she was back on her old full-time basis as a ballerina.

Although pretty, vivacious Marjorie admits that she has her hands full, she is delighted both with babies and ballet. Asked how she so successfully manages her dual career, Marjorie Tallchief—Mrs. George Skibine—has a ready answer: "It will work only if both husband and wife are dancers!" George Skibine agrees wholeheartedly with his talented young wife, and adds, with an amused grin, that she seems to have proved that you can have your cake and eat it too!

Tamara Toumanova

GLAMOROUS, exotic Tamara Toumanova has lived a life full of adulation, fame, and drama in rich abundance. Even her birth was dramatic. One wintry day in 1919, the Princess Eugenie Toumanova and her husband, a Czarist officer, made their perilous escape from the Russian Revolution in a boxcar headed for Siberia. Somewhere along the way, in that cold and crowded boxcar, the baby Tamara, who was to become one of the most famous dancers in the world, was born.

After long and weary wanderings, the little family settled in Paris, where they lived the desperate hand-to-mouth existence that was the lot of most refugees. Tamara, a wisp of a child, was always dancing, and her parents decided they must somehow manage to have her properly taught. Scraping together enough money for a few lessons, they took her to the famed Russian ballet teacher, Mme Olga Preobrajenska. The five-year-old child danced for Madame, showing such extraordinary grace that she was immediately accepted as a pupil.

Day after day the little tot practiced at the *barre*, amazing her teacher with her progress. Then one day the famous ballerina Anna Pavlova came to visit her old friend Preobrajenska, and chanced to see little Tamara dance. Struck by the child's bright beauty and talent, Pavlova took her under her wing, and featured her in one of her own performances at the Paris Trocadero. The little girl, with her great dark eyes and enchanting smile, created a delighted stir, and was taken up as a sort of pet by Paris society, much in demand for parties and receptions. Her parents allowed her to dance at these affairs only occasionally, even though they were in desperate need of the money she brought home.

Preobrajenska, who foresaw a brilliant future for her young prodigy, took special pains with her training, continuing to give her daily lessons when her family could no longer afford them. When Tamara was ten, her teacher invited a group of critics to watch her dance. This informal recital led to Tamara's being invited to dance at the Paris Opéra as the star in a children's ballet— the youngest guest artist ever to be so honored.

Three years later George Balanchine, choreographer for the De Basil Ballet Russe de Monte Carlo, saw the dazzlingly beautiful young Tamara at work at Preobrajenska's studio and promptly offered her a contract with the De Basil company.

Tamara started right at the top in her first professional job, as one of the company's three leading ballerinas. They were a lovely trio, all three so young that De Basil billed them as "The Baby Ballerinas:" Tamara Toumanova, thirteen, vivid and dramatic; Tatiana Riabouchinska, fourteen, blonde and elfin; and Irina Baronova, thirteen, fair and sweetly feminine. A rivalry developed almost instantly between Tamara and Irina, though it was Tamara who scored the first successes. In *Cotillon* and *Concurrence*, which Balanchine created especially to show her off, and as the Top in Massine's *Jeux d'Enfants*, Tamara displayed the dazzling personality and technique which have since made her a box-office sensation the world over.

From the night of their opening in Monte Carlo in 1932, The Baby Ballerinas were the darlings of Europe. Admirers all over the continent were agog at their fresh beauty and amazing technique, and flocked to the stage door to catch a glimpse of them—and had to be content with just a glimpse, so carefully were these prodigies chaperoned.

The Baby Ballerinas invaded America in December 1933, and took New York by storm. Americans had never seen anything like the amazing *pirouettes* and *fouettés* that these girls did with such charming ease. Tamara, widely publicized as "The Black Pearl" because of her raven-haired beauty, toured the United States, Europe, and Australia with the company for the next seven years, starring in *Petrouchka, Swan Lake, Les Sylphides, Le Beau Danube,* and *Choreartium.* She left the company briefly in 1938 to dance in

TAMARA TOUMANOVA

in the *Dying Swan* from the motion picture *Tonight We Sing*

the musical, *Stars in Your Eyes,* and by this time found American
life so much to her liking that she stayed in New York when the
company left at the end of the 1940 season for an extended tour of
South America.

Meanwhile, Hollywood had discovered ballet. Toumanova
was starred in a film version of the ballet *Capriccio Espagnol,* released under the title *Spanish Festival.* Her aristocratic beauty
proved so photogenic that she was persuaded to remain in Hollywood to make another movie in 1943, *Days of Glory,* in which she
starred with Gregory Peck in her first straight acting role.

Immediately after the release of that movie, Toumanova married its director, Casey Robinson, a top-notch producer with Twentieth Century-Fox Films.

She appeared as guest artist with Ballet Theatre in 1944 and 1945—her last important appearances in the United States. Probably the most world-traveled of all ballerinas, she has since danced in Europe, South America, Africa, Egypt, and Scandinavia with her own company, and as guest artist with De Cuevas Grand Ballet, the London Festival Ballet, and La Scala in Milan. Every summer, she appears as guest artist at the Paris Opéra.

No matter how heavy her schedule, or how tempting the worldwide offers, Toumanova always heads for home in November of each year, to spend the holidays with her husband and her mother in their lavish Beverly Hills home. One such holiday homecoming in 1952 led to her playing the part of the great Anna Pavlova in the movie, *Tonight We Sing*, which her husband directed. It was remarkably fitting that she should have been chosen for this role, not only because of her deeply moving beauty as a dancer, but also because she has idolized Pavlova ever since their meeting so many years ago.

Tamara Toumanova is a dancer of extraordinary power, excelling in dramatic roles and in those which call for her almost acrobatic virtuosity. For sheer dramatic force, her wicked Odile in *Swan Lake* is unsurpassed. In all the great classic *pas de deux*—*Don Quixote, Blue Bird, Magic Swan*—she is at her exciting best, for they exactly suit her vivid temperament and dazzling technique.

Toumanova has been known by many titles: "Boxcar Baby," "Baby Ballerina," "The Black Pearl,"—even "The Sexiest Classical Ballerina" (bestowed on her by ballet photographer Baron). But the title she wears with the greatest pride and delight is the one accompanying the *Grand Prix de Giselle*, awarded her in 1952, which honors her as "the greatest classical ballerina in Europe."

Oleg Tupine

I F OLEG TUPINE had had his own way, he never would have become a dancer. As a boy in Paris, he wanted to be an engineer, or possibly a professional athlete, or even an army officer, like his father. But one day when he was fourteen, his mother announced: "I have made up my mind. You are going to be a dancer."

Her reason was an entirely practical one. She was determined that her sons should not know the same financial insecurity that she and her husband had known. As Russian refugees they had wandered homeless for years. Their first son, Oleg, had been born aboard ship off Istanbul in 1920, their second son two years later in Bulgaria. The boys had been raised in Paris, and now that they were old enough it was time for them to start training for a career. Dancing was one of the few uncrowded professions in refugee-filled Paris, and her sons, who were both handsome, athletic boys, could earn a good living at it.

Oleg and his brother went unhappily to ballet class, filled with resentment at the ridiculous exercises that forced them to give up their usual after-school ball games. They hated the long daily trip to Mme Egorova's studio, far on the other side of Paris.

After Oleg had studied three years with Mme Egorova, she arranged for him to dance with the Ballets de la Jeunesse. Seventeen-year-old Oleg had a schedule that was almost too much for him. In addition to his daily ballet lessons, he was working intently toward graduation examinations at high school, and rehearsing every night until one a.m. for his roles with the Ballets. Every morning he got up at six o'clock and started all over again.

In spite of trying to be in three places at once that whole year, Oleg managed to graduate from high school with honors. Turning his back forever on his ambition to be an engineer, he reluctantly accepted a job with the Original Ballet Russe in London.

It took only one season, dancing in the *corps de ballet,* for him to realize, with surprise, that he was actually enjoying being a dancer. A year-long tour to Australia followed, after which he knew with certainty that ballet was a career which he would happily follow the rest of his life.

The company was barely back in Paris before the dancers were told to pack their bags for a tour of Germany. On August 31, 1939, as Oleg entered the Paris station to catch the Berlin Express, he saw the headlines all Europe had been dreading: "HITLER MARCHES INTO POLAND." The German tour was canceled.

The Original Ballet Russe went to New York instead. From there young Oleg went on with them for a four-year tour of Mexico and South America. He danced his first solo in *Prince Igor* in 1942.

His second solo, the *Blue Bird pas de deux,* Oleg danced on exactly twenty-four hours' notice. He rehearsed for thirteen solid hours, and was completely exhausted by curtain time. To this day, he has no idea how he got through the performance. All he remembers is the wild applause that greeted him when it was over.

Most dancers, Tupine says, have had the same sort of experience. He himself once danced the role of the Prince in *Swan Lake* with a broken kneecap. He was quite unconscious of pain while he was dancing, but the minute the performance was over he couldn't walk a step. Dancers learn a kind of mind-over-body mastery, he says, that often enables them to perform in the face of incredible odds.

Tupine made his debut as a *premier danseur* in 1944, in Buenos Aires as Prince Charming in *Aurora's Wedding.*

He played the leading role in another wedding the following year—his own. He had courted pretty, Hollywood-born Nathalie Conlon, a member of the company's *corps de ballet,* all over South America, and when they reached Venezuela they were married.

During the rest of the tour Tupine danced one role after another, with tremendous success in *Les Sylphides, Spectre de la Rose, Firebird,* and *Cain and Abel.*

He danced with the Markova-Dolin Company in 1948, and

OLEG TUPINE and YVETTE CHAUVIRÉ in *Romeo and Juliet*

the following year he and his wife joined the Ballet Russe de Monte Carlo—Tupine as *premier danseur,* and his wife (whose professional name is Natalia Clare) as soloist. In that company Tupine's fame as a classical *premier danseur* has grown with each passing year. His tall, broad-shouldered grace and romantic charm make his *Romeo and Juliet* and his Prince in *Swan Lake* especially memorable.

The ballets Tupine most enjoys, he says, are the ones in which his wife dances too. "Nathalie and I are entirely different, but we complement each other perfectly." Offstage they share the same interests and enthusiasms. They enjoy spending Saturday afternoons at the ball park. They play bridge. They have a host of friends, especially in Hollywood, where they spend most of their time between seasons with Nathalie's parents. During some of these Hollywood vacations Tupine has danced in two movies: *Look for the Silver Lining* and *The Great Waltz.*

Tupine is an intelligent, practical, thoroughly likable man who does not let his career as a *premier danseur* preoccupy him to the exclusion of wider interests. He is an astute businessman, a well-informed student of world affairs, and a linguist of considerable ability.

Oleg and Nathalie are parents of a son, Alexis, who was born in 1951. On short tours of the Ballet Russe, they take Alex along, and he is showered with attention and affection by the whole company. When anyone asks Tupine if his son is going to be a dancer, he replies emphatically that Alex will decide for himself when the time comes. But with a daughter, he hastens to add, it would be different! "I should *insist* that she take ballet lessons, because they develop poise, elegance, and grace."

Jocelyn Vollmar

U P UNTIL a few short years ago, young Jocelyn Vollmar had never been out of California. Today she travels the world over as one of the leading ballerinas in the De Cuevas Grand Ballet. Her life, she says, is like a daydream come true.

Jocelyn, born in San Francisco in 1925, had her first ballet instruction when she was five, with her mother, a former actress and dancer. When she was twelve, she enrolled at the San Francisco School of Ballet where, because her mother had trained her so thoroughly, she was soon put into the advanced class. This starry-eyed child lived only for the days of her ballet lessons—the days between seemed interminable. There was always something wonderful going on at the school. Best of all were the days when she could watch the rehearsals of the San Francisco Opera Ballet, and its petite star, Janet Reed, whom little Jocelyn adored.

Delicate, idealistic Jocelyn was completely absorbed in her training, and showed talent and aptitude that soon began to single her out.

She had been at the school little more than a year when she was chosen as an extra for the visiting Ballet Russe company's performance of *Scheherazade.* Jocelyn reported backstage at the San Francisco Opera House for rehearsal, feeling as if she were in one of her favorite daydreams. Actually rehearsing the wild finale of *Scheherazade* with real ballet dancers, she knew rapturously that this was no dream! Her only fear was that she might forget the strange dancers between whom she was to dance, so she carefully memorized their faces. But on the evening of the actual performance, when all the dancers appeared in costume, Jocelyn found to her terror that she could not find her partners, now disguised by their heavy make-up. What would she do? Then, out of nowhere, two dancers seized her by the hands and swung her into the dance

"To this day," she says now, "I shall never know with whom or what I was dancing. I know only that suddenly it was all finished—neatly and in place!"

Jocelyn was in her third year of training when the San Francisco Opera Ballet left for a short tour of the West Coast. The young student went along as a temporary member of the *corps de ballet*, and had a brief taste of life as a professional dancer, convincing her that this was the life she wanted.

She danced her first solo, Mazurka in *Les Sylphides*, when she was seventeen. Three years later, in 1945, she danced her first ballerina role—Odile in the *Black Swan pas de deux*, which won her the place as principal dancer of the San Francisco Ballet. Local ballet-goers flocked to see their lovely, dark-haired ballerina in the great classics, and applauded her especially in the lead roles of Wil- lam Christensen's own ballets, *Pyramus and Thisbe* and *Winter Carnival*.

For a while Jocelyn wondered earnestly if she could possibly squeeze in a college education along with ballet. But finally she faced the inevitable fact that a career in ballet left no time for a regular college education. She compromised by buying a "five-foot shelf" of the classics, and has been determinedly reading through them ever since. A spirited, unusually pretty girl, Jocelyn couldn't pass up all "dates," nor could she completely do without her two favorite sports, hiking and swimming. She continued her piano lessons, and kept her hand in at her favorite domestic pastime, baking cakes—"the fancier and gooier, the better!"

The New York City Ballet invited her to join the company in 1948. After her successful year with them, she spent the next two years with Ballet Theatre, adding immeasurably to her reputation as a dancer. The Marquis de Cuevas, having seen this young and unusually talented ballerina, persuaded her to join his company in Paris late in 1950. On tour in Africa, a scant two years later, Jocelyn Vollmar, the girl from San Francisco, saw her name go up on the posters as a star with the De Cuevas Grand Ballet.

JOCELYN VOLLMAR in *Paquita*

Igor Youskevitch

To THE dreaming, haunting refrain of Chopin's music, fragile sylphs wafted through the moonlit glade of *Les Sylphides.* Backstage, a harassed electrician worried his blue spotlights, trying to keep his mechanical moonlight centered on the floating dancers. Suddenly a tall figure in white tights and black velvet tunic catapulted into the glade, soaring halfway across the stage in two flying leaps. The audience, left gasping, burst into spontaneous applause. The electrician, his spotlights momentarily forgotten, beamed at his assistant with satisfaction: "That Youskevitch! He gets 'em every time with those leaps of his!"

Igor Youskevitch has always had an amazing technical agility. All during his school years he was an outstanding athlete and gymnast, and at Belgrade Royal University was elected to the Sokol, an international organization of gymnasts. Like David Lichine, he calls ballet the most strenuous, demanding, and precise of all forms of athletics.

Igor, the son of a judge, was born in 1912 in Pyriatin, Russia, and moved to Yugoslavia when he was a small boy. He was nineteen when he first decided on ballet as a career. From the day he entered ballet school in Belgrade, he put all other interests aside, and progressed so rapidly that inside of a year he was a professional dancer, partnering the young Yugoslav dancer, Xenia Grunt, on a concert tour of Europe.

When their tour ended in Paris, he stayed there to study with Mme Olga Preobrajenṣka, who gave him the intensive training and constructive criticism he wanted. After two years with Preobrajenṣka, he became a soloist with Nijinska's *Théâtre de Danse,* and just one year later rose to the rank of *premier danseur* with Leon Woicikowski's Ballet.

He joined the Ballet Russe de Monte Carlo in 1937, and when

IGOR YOUSKEVITCH, *premier danseur*

the company opened in Paris that fall, critics called it the most brilliant company that had been seen since the earliest days of the Diaghilev Ballets Russes thirty years before. Paris went wild over its stars: Massine, Toumanova, and Danilova, and was agape at the breathtaking dancing of the youngest *premier danseur*, Igor Youskevitch.

Youskevitch won his full share of the general acclaim as he toured with the company through Europe and the United States for the next four years. His phenomenal technique, particularly apparent in *Spectre de la Rose*, was only a part of his brilliance. Audiences thrilled to the virility of his dancing, and were irresistibly drawn by the warm magnetism of his personality. One of his former partners recently remarked: "Youskevitch is a wonderful partner, because he dances with his heart."

His career was interrupted in 1944 when he joined the U. S. Navy as a Specialist, Second Class. When he was dropped back into civilian life two years later, he discovered to his surprise that Navy life had added twenty-five pounds to his normally lean figure. Dismayed, because being overweight is a disaster for any dancer, he set about getting himself back in dancing condition at once, for he was soon to appear as guest artist with Massine's Ballet Russe Highlights. He set himself a strenuous, rigid schedule of diet and exercise, around which his whole household revolved. His wife, the former dancer Anna Scarpova (whom he married in London in 1938) did all she could to help him. She saw to it that he kept to his starch-free, energy-building diet; she became a combination business manager and social secretary, leaving him entirely free to concentrate on his work. He lost the twenty-five pounds in almost as many days, and was in top dancing form once more when he reported to the Massine company for the summer season.

That fall he appeared with Ballet Theatre for the first time. *Premier danseur* with that company for many ensuing seasons, his brilliant partnering of ballerina Alicia Alonso in the great *pas de deux* and in such classics as *Princess Aurora* was the eagerly awaited highlight of each performance both in the United States and Europe.

His apparently inexhaustible energy and resilience are a source of wonder to everyone. His secret may be that when he has a few minutes to relax he makes the most of them. In his dressing-room before he goes on he is the picture of complete lethargy as he sits slumped in a chair. If anyone asks him how he feels, he invariably and wearily replies: "I'm tired!" Yet five minutes later he leaps on stage—electrifying the audience with the incredible ease of his *grand jetés* and *entrechats*.

His between-season summers are spent in a variety of activities. The summer of 1948 he was in Cuba as *premier danseur* in the new company that his good friends Alicia and Fernando Alonso had just started. In 1952 he went to London to make a movie, *Invitation to the Dance*, with ballerinas Tamara Toumanova and Diana Adams. In other summers, when he needs a vacation from dancing, he sets off with a couple of cronies for a week or two of his favorite sport—deep-sea fishing. Summer or winter, wherever he is, he likes an occasional relaxing game of poker, at which his friends have found, to their sorrow, that he is very good—"and quite apt to clean us all out!"

Premier danseur Youskevitch is a devoted father, liking nothing better than a chance to talk about his young daughter, Maria. When she was in kindergarten in New York, Maria begged so earnestly to learn to dance that her father and mother began her first lessons at home. By the time she was in the first grade, Maria was something of a celebrity in her public school. Her whole class, awed by the fact that her father was a famous dancer and that Maria herself was learning to dance, wanted to take ballet too. As a result, Maria's mother offered to give them lessons, and the class that Mrs. Youskevitch started became a regular part of the school curriculum.

Youskevitch was delighted with this turn of events, because, he says, only by active participation does a child gain an understanding of any art. It doesn't matter whether any of these moppets become dancers—the important thing is that they will have gained an appreciation of ballet which will make them the perceptive audiences of tomorrow.

George Zoritch

BALLET-GOERS shook their heads regretfully, some years ago, when talented George Zoritch gave up a promising career as *premier danseur* and went into movies and musicals instead. It was a shame, they agreed, that his vigor and versatility were lost to ballet. But today, after having staged an almost unprecedented comeback, George Zoritch dances again in ballet—one of the brightest of its international stars.

Born in Moscow in 1917, and christened Yuri (Russian for George), he grew up in Kovno, Lithuania. Ballet was just a word to him until, on his eleventh birthday, his grandmother took him to see *Coppélia*. After the performance he went directly home where he jumped about the family living-room in wild attempts at imitating the wonderful leaps and turns he had seen. Day after day, he kept it up until, he says, he became a "menace to the furniture."

Almost in self-defense, his family enrolled him at the ballet school in Kovno, where he proved to have such an instinctive flair for dancing that his instructor could not believe he had never studied before. Practically at once, he was put into the Children's Ballet of Kovno, and made his debut in *The Nutcracker* that same year—a very satisfying performance, from young Yuri's point of view. Ballet, he decided, was definitely for him!

When he was sixteen, he arrived in Paris to begin his studies with the famous Mme Olga Preobrajenska, and in less than a year was a professional dancer. Before his eighteenth birthday, enterprising young Yuri had gained an impressive amount of experience in the *corps de ballet* of three companies: the Ida Rubenstein Company in Paris, the Victor Dandré Company,* touring the Far East and Australia, and Nijinska's *Théâtre de Danse*.

---

* Victor Dandré was the widower of the legendary Anna Pavlova.

GEORGE ZORITCH dances *Scherzo* with DENISE BOURGEOIS

Yuri was eighteen when he set out for London, where he was taken into the brilliant new De Basil Ballet Russe as a soloist. Very shortly afterward he won his first *premier danseur* role in Massine's *Jardin Public.*

Yuri's flashing dark good looks and remarkable versatility won him immediate notice with the Ballet Russe. When he danced the spectacular leads in *Afternoon of a Faun* and *Spectre de la Rose,* he was wildly acclaimed not only for his astonishing virtuosity but also for the subtlety of his interpretation. He toured Europe and America with the Ballet Russe de Monte Carlo for the next five years, dancing brilliantly in the classics, and winning high praise for his Mercury in *Seventh Symphony* and his Baron in *Gaité Parisienne*.

But those five years had been a constant, exhausting struggle. Yuri was tired of the endless competition for top roles; he was tired of the continued travel, and of the shoestring salary. It was while the company was in New York that Yuri suddenly found himself "fed up," as he puts it, with the whole ballet business.

He landed a part in a Broadway musical, *Early to Bed*, and was perfectly happy during the twenty-six months of its successful run. In this musical he had a chance to act as well as dance, and says today with a grin: "I liked having lines to speak. It's the ham in me!"

After playing in two other musicals, *The Merry Widow* and *Rhapsody*, Yuri took off on another tangent, which led to Hollywood. He made three movies: *Night and Day, Escape Me Never,* and *The Unfinished Dance,* and stayed on the West Coast to dance in the light-opera revivals of *Louisiana Purchase, Die Fledermaus* and *The Great Waltz*.

His next venture took him back to New York, where he did the choreography for a television production of *Cinderella*. After that, he had a short fling in an Olsen and Johnson extravaganza, *Pardon My French*.

Yuri had been away from ballet proper for nine years, when suddenly he was "fed up" again, and homesick for ballet. At whatever cost, he resolved, he *must* get back into top-notch dancing condition and join a ballet company. It would be extraordinarily difficult, he knew, for if a dancer misses just one week it is noticeable in his dancing. He sailed for Paris, put himself into the hands of his first teacher, Preobrajenska, and worked with unflagging determination.

Early in 1951, Zoritch became a *premier danseur* with the De Cuevas Grand Ballet. Critics promptly hailed him as one of the most exciting dancers in Europe. Prodigal son George Zoritch was back home in ballet.

Some Ballet Terms

AND WHAT THEY MEAN

THE DANCERS IN BALLET

corps de ballet (kor de ba-**lay**) A group of dancers who dance together—the equivalent of a chorus. Sometimes called the ensemble.

soloist A dancer who dances solo roles, either alone or in a group of not more than four.

ballerina (bal-e-**ree**-na) A female dancer who regularly dances leading roles in a company's repertoire.

prima ballerina (**pree**-ma bal-e-**ree**-na) The first or principal ballerina in a company. The term is not too frequently used.

prima ballerina assoluta Formerly, a title conferred officially in pre-war Russia on the one dancer who, above all others, was outstanding in a generation. Today, it is used more loosely (but very infrequently) by critics who want to pay a great ballerina the highest possible tribute. Danilova, Markova, Chauviré, and Fonteyn, in contemporary ballet, have been so honored.

premier danseur (prem-**yay** dahn-**ser**) The first or principal male dancer of a company—partner of the ballerina. Sometimes a dancer with particularly elegant technique, of the classic Russian system, is called a *premier danseur noble*.

OTHER PEOPLE CONNECTED WITH BALLET

ballet master (or *mistress*) The person who is in charge of the dancers in a company, and responsible for rehearsing ballets, assigning roles, and conducting classes for the dancers.

choreographer (koh-ree-**og**-raffer) A person who composes the dance movements and patterns of a ballet, and arranges them to fit the music which has been selected.

impresario The person financially responsible for a ballet company's appearances. He may merely engage different companies at different times, or may own or direct one company.

TERMS USED IN DANCING

adagio (a-**dah**-jo) The opening part of the classic *pas de deux*, danced by the ballerina and her partner. The *adagio* is interrupted by variations in which each dances a solo.

arabesque (ar-a-**besk**) There are several kinds of arabesques, all of them based on the classic pose in which a dancer stands on one leg with the other leg extended behind her, one arm extended front and the other back.

barre (bar) Or practice *barre*. A fixed wooden rail, approximately waist-high, used in class by pupils and dancers to steady them and help maintain balance during exercises.

[173]

balletomane (ba-**let**-o-mane) A ballet enthusiast or "fan." Formerly the term meant someone well-informed on ballet and a connoisseur of technique, but now it can mean anyone who is a regular ballet-goer.

cabriole (cab-ree-**ohl**) A jump in which the legs are almost parallel to the floor, with the lower leg beating against the upper leg.

divertissement (dee-vair-tees-**mah**) A group of dances interpolated into a classic ballet, where they are sometimes called *entrées,* for displaying individual dancers in separate numbers, often of spectacular nature.

elevation The height from the floor which a dancer can attain in a leap.

entrechat (ahn-tre-**sha**) A jump during which the legs cross quickly, front and back, once or many times while in the air. *Entrechat six,* quite common in contemporary ballet, means three crossings of the legs while in the air.

extension Stretching of the leg, knee straight, at any angle to the body.

fouetté (foo-ay-**tay**) A whipped step. *Fouetté en tournant*—A series of turns on one foot; the other leg, circling rapidly, whips the body around.

jeté (zheh-**tay**) A small jump in any direction from one foot to the other.

    grand jeté (**grahn** zheh-**tay**) A big leap in any direction from one foot to the other.

line The outline of a dancer's body while she is dancing or holding a pose. The proportions of a dancer's body, the straightness of legs and back, the carriage of the head, curve of the arms, and good *turn-out,* all are integral parts of the true classic *line.*

pas de deux (pa de **der**) A dance for two.

pas de trois (pa de **trwa**) A dance for three.

pas de quatre (pa de **katr**) A dance for four.

pirouette (peer-oo-**et**) A complete turn of the body on one leg from any position, ending in the same position in which the dancer began. Multiple pirouettes can be dazzling in effect.

plié (plee-**ay**) A bending of the knees with the feet on the floor. In ballet class, the purpose of the *plié* is to stretch and strengthen the muscles and tendons of the feet and legs. In dancing, the *plié* becomes the dancer's springboard— to begin and end a jump.

    demi-plié (**dem**-ee plee-**ay**) A half-bend of the knees with the feet flat on the floor.

    grand plié (**grahn** plee-**ay**) A full bend of the knees, on half-toe or *en pointes.*

pointes (pwant) Or *en pointes,* or *sur les pointes.* On the tips of the toes. Only female dancers dance *en pointes*—giving the illusion of flight and of lightness.

turn-out The turning out of the leg from the hip, so that the whole leg is at right angles to the body. The *turned-out* position enables the dancer to move legs and feet with greater ease.

tutu (**tu-tu**) The female dancer's traditional costume, with a stiff, many-layered skirt.

    romantic tutu The long tutu, just above ankle-length, worn in Romantic Ballets.

    classic tutu The short tutu, varying from knee-length to just below the hips, worn in Classic Ballets.

Index

Adams, Diana, 4–6, 91, 169
Adams, Mrs. Emily Hadley, 4
Alonso (ah-**lon**-zo), Alicia (ah-**lee**-see-ah), 7–11, 168, 169
Alonso, Fernando, 7, 8, 10–11, 169
Alonso, Laurita, 8, 10, 11
American Ballet Company, 16, 51, 82, 87
Anchutina, Leda, 48, 51
Anna Pavlova Company, 98
Ashton, Frederick, 59, 62, 88, 112
Astafieva, Seraphima, 42, 44, 110

Babilée (bab-ee-**lay**), Jean (jhahn), 12–15, 96, 99, 104, 124
Balanchine, George, 5, 39, 82, 94–5, 102, 111, 116, 150, 154, 156
Ballet Alicia Alonso, 7, 11
Ballet Caravan, 10, 16, 18, 86
Ballet de la Ville des Anges, 100
Ballet Russe de Monte Carlo, 18, 26, 28, 29, 32, 34, 40, 51, 62, 64, 74–6, 98, 103, 113, 115, 116, 118, 120, 122, 132, 146, 148, 152, 162, 166, 171
Ballet Society, 94, 150
Ballet Theatre, 4, 5, 10, 11, 15, 32, 46, 51, 76, 80–3, 86, 87, 90, 91, 99, 106, 113, 118, 128, 130, 134, 142, 143, 152, 158, 164, 168
Ballets de Paris, 77, 106, 107, 126
Ballets de la Jeunesse, 140, 159
Ballets Russes, 42, 45, 46. *See also* Ballet Russe de Monte Carlo, Diaghilev Ballets Russes
Ballet Variant, 144
Baronova, Irina, 51, 132, 156
Belcher, Ernest, 28, 147, 152
Bentley, Muriel, 91
Bérard, Christian, 142
Blum, René, 50–1, 142
Bolm, Adolph, 28, 133
Boris, Ruthanna, 16–8
Bourgeois (boor-**jwah**), Denise (deh-**nees**), 171

Camargo Society, 46, 112
Caron (ka-rohn), Leslie, 19–22, 96, 99, 124, 125
Cecchetti, Enrico, 44, 102, 111
Chappell, William, 60
Chase, Lucia, 76, 82
Chauviré (show-vee-**ray**), Yvette (ee-**vet**), 23–7, 103, 104, 146, 161
Chicago Civic Opera Ballet, 84, 86
Children's Ballet of Kovno, 170
Children's Ballet of Warsaw, 120
Chouteau (shoo-**toh**), Yvonne (ee-**von**), 28–30
Christensen, Willam, 128, 164
Christensen, Lew, 18
Chujoy, Anatole, 94, 118
Clare, Natalia, 160, 162
Cocteau (kok-**toh**), Jean (zhahn), 14
Couat, Mlle, 23
Craske, Margaret, 90

Dance Theatre, London, 90
Danielian (dah-**nee**-lee-an), Leon (**lay**-on), 10, 30, 31–4, 121

Danilova (dah-**nee**-loh-vah), Alexandra, **28**–9, 32, 35–41, 45, 50, 51, 56, 62, 75, 110, **115**, 122, 146, 168
Daydé (day-day), Liane (lee-**ann**), 104
de Basil, Col., 40, 50, 132
De Basil's Ballet Russe de Monte Carlo, 46, 50, 77, 98, 131, 142, 146, 156, 171. *See also* Original Ballet Russe
de Cuevas, Marquis, 76, 154, 164
De Cuevas Grand Ballet, 51, 76, 143, 147, 152, 154, 158, 163, 164, 172
de Mille, Agnes, 4, 90, 114
de Valois (de-va-**lwah**), Ninette (nee-**net**), 45, 46, 58, 70, 114
Diaghilev (**dyah**-gee-lyef), Serge (sairzh), 39, 40, 42, 44, 46, 102, 104, 110–12
Diaghilev Ballets Russes, 39, 44, 102, 108, 135, 140, 168
Dolin (**doh**-lin), Anton, 42–7, 61–2, 106, 110, 112, 113, 152
Dolin's Festival Ballet, 26, 113
Dollar, William, 18

Eglevsky (ee-**glef**-skee), André (ahn-dray), 48–51, 151, 152
Egorova, Lubov, 44, 98, 159

Federova (feh-**deh**-roh-vah), Alexandra, 10
Festival Ballet, 46, 99–100, 106, 134
Fifield, Elaine, 52–4
Fokine, Michel, 82
Fonteyn (fon-**tayn**), Margot (mar-goh), **55**–60, 65, 66, 70, 72, 73, 75, 108, 136
Franklin, Frederic, 35, 61–4, 75, 146

Gotovzeva (got-of-tsay-vah), Lydia, 36
Grey, Beryl, 65–8
Grunt, Xenia, 166

Haskell, Arnold, 26, 47, 59, 72, 80
Helpmann, Robert, 69–73, 138
Hightower, Rosella, 74–6, 90
Huston, John, 106
Hurok, Sol, 142

Ida Rubenstein Company, 98, 170
Imperial School of Ballet, 36
International Ballet, 136

Jeanmaire (jhahn-**mare**), Renée (re-**nay**), 23, 77–9, 123, 124, 126

Karsavina, Tamara, 36
Kaye, Danny, 78
Kaye, Nora, 10, 51, 80–3, 90, 108
Kelly, Gene, 6, 20
Kennedy, Ludovic, 139
Kniaseff (knee-ah-sef), Boris, 24
Kochno, Boris, 124
Koesun, Ruth Ann, 87
Kriza (**kree**-za), John, 10, 84–7

Laing (lang), Hugh, 3, 5, 6, 82, 88–9, 112, 143
Lanchbery, John, 54
Lang, Harold, 86
LeClercq (le-**clair**), Jacques, 92
LeClercq (le-**clair**), Tanaquil (tah-ne-keel), 51, 92–5

Legat, Nicholas, 61, 136
Leon Woicikowski's Ballet, 50, 166
Les Ballets de Paris, 59, 77, 126
Les Ballets des Champs-Élysées, 12, 14, 15, 19, 20, 22, 33, 34, 77, 96, 99, 124-6
Lichine (li-sheen), David, 19, 96-100, 131, 134, 152, 166
Lifar (lee-far), Serge (sairzh), 24, 44, 62, 77, 101-4, 105-6, 113
London Ballet, 90
London Festival Ballet, 158
Loring, Eugene, 18
Lyon, Annabelle, 82

Marchand (mar-shahn), Colette (coh-let), 23, 105-7, 124, 126
Markova (mar-koh-va), Alicia (ah-lee-see-ah), 42, 45, 46, 47, 51, 56, 58, 70, 75, 88, 90-1, 108-14, 141, 143, 146, 152
Markova-Dolin Ballet, 46, 62, 76, 113, 160
Martinez, Alicia. See Alonso, Alicia
Martin, John, 114, 147, 151
"Mary Ellen." See Moylan, Mary Ellen
Massine, Leonide, 29, 32, 62, 75, 90, 135, 138, 156, 168, 171
Massine's Ballet Russe Highlights, 76, 143, 168
Metropolitan Ballet, London, 106
Metropolitan Opera Ballet Company, N. Y., 16
Metropolitan Opera Ballet School, N. Y., 82
Metropolitan Opera House, N. Y., 3, 5, 55, 62, 80, 82, 86, 90
Miss Thorne's Dancing Academy, 108
Moncion, Francisco, 94, 149
Mordkin Ballet, 8, 10
Mordkin Ballet School, 32, 92
Mordkin, Mikhail, 32
Moylan, Mary Ellen, 115-18

Nepo, Constantin, 27
New Opera Company, 116
New York City Ballet, 3, 6, 18, 48, 51, 83, 91, 92, 94, 130, 147, 150, 164
Nijinska, Bronislava, 44, 98, 101-2, 148, 152
Nijinska's Théâtre de Danse, 166, 170
Nijinski, Vaslav, 15, 36
Nouveau Ballet de Monte Carlo, 26, 77, 103
Novak (no-vak), Nina (nee-nah), 119-22

Original Ballet Russe, 32, 51, 76, 113, 143, 154, 159, 160

Page, Ruth, 84
Paris Opéra, 15, 23, 24, 26, 27, 101, 102-4, 105, 124, 150, 156, 158
Paris Opéra Ballet Company, 77-8
Paris Opéra Ballet School, 12, 77, 105, 124
Pavlova (pav-lo-va), Anna, 26, 36, 56, 61, 69-70, 99, 113, 155, 158, 170
Perkins School of the Dance, 74
Petit (peh-tee), Margaret, 19
Petit (peh-tee), Roland, 12, 15, 19, 77, 78, 79, 106, 107, 123-6
Philippart, Nathalie, 12, 14, 15
Polish Opera Ballet School, 120

Polish State Ballet, 122
Preobrajenska (pre-o-bra-zhain-ska), Olga, 90, 132, 140, 155-6, 166, 170, 172
Pruzina, Mme, 61
René Blum Ballet de Monte Carlo, 50-1, 142
Rambert, Marie, 88, 112
Rambert's Ballet Club, 90
Rambert's ballet school, 88
Reed, Janet, 127-30, 163
Riabouchinska (ree-ah-boo-shin-ska), Tatiana (tat-zi-ah-na), 96, 97, 98, 131-4, 156
Robbins, Jerome, 86
Roland Petit's Ballets de Paris, 106
Royal Academy of Dancing, 52, 101
Royal Danish Ballet, 59
Royal Opera House, London, 138
Russian State Ballet, 38
Russian State Dancers, 39

Sadler's Wells Ballet, 45, 46, 52, 54, 55, 65, 72, 73, 77, 113, 137, 138
Sadler's Wells Ballet School, 52, 56-7, 66, 70, 135, 136
Sadler's Wells Theatre, 66, 136
San Francisco Opera Ballet, 127, 128, 163, 164
San Francisco School of the Ballet, 163
Scarpova, Anna, 168, 169
School of American Ballet, 16, 28, 82, 92-3, 115
Shearer, Moira (moy-rah), 72, 78, 135-9
Skibine (skee-bean), George, 90, 140-3, 152, 153, 154
Skibine, Mrs. George. See Tallchief, Marjorie
Slavenska-Franklin Ballet, 64, 146
Slavenska (slah-ven-skah), Mia (mee-ah), 35, 64, 103, 144-6
Spessivtzeva, Olga, 44, 46
Stone, Bentley, 84
Studio Centrale d'État, 101

Tallchief, Maria, 51, 92, 147-51, 152
Tallchief, Marjorie, 143, 147, 152-5
Toumanova (too-man-oh-vah), Tamara (tah-mah-rah), 51, 62, 99, 132, 152, 155-8, 168, 169
Toye, Wendy, 61
Trefilova, Vera, 44
Tudor, Antony, 4, 5, 30, 80, 82, 88, 90, 91, 112
Tupine (teeyou-pin), Oleg (oh-leg), 26, 117, 118, 159-62

Vic-Wells Ballet, 46, 113
Vic-Wells Company, 70
Victor Dandré Company, 170
Vladimiroff, Pierre, 44, 82
Volinine, 19, 50
Vollmar, Jocelyn, 163-5
Vyroubova (vee-roo-boh-vah), Nina, 124

Williamson, Audrey, 73

Youskevitch (yous-kay-vitch), Igor (ee-gor), 62, 75, 143, 166-9

Zagreb National Opera Ballet School, 146
Zoritch, George, 170-2

The text of this book is set in Linotype Caledonia, designed by W. A. Dwiggins, distinguished American typographer and type designer. Composed, printed, and bound by Kingsport Press, Inc., Kingsport, Tennessee. Engravings by Capper Engraving Company, Inc., Knoxville, Tennessee.